NEW PERSPECTIVES ON RETAILING AND STORE PATRONAGE BEHAVIOR

INTERNATIONAL STUDIES IN ENTREPRENEURSHIP

Series Editors:
Zoltan J. Acs
University of Baltimore
Baltimore, Maryland USA

David B. Audretsch
Indiana University
Bloomington, Indiana USA

Other books in the series:

NEW PERSPECTIVES ON RETAILING AND STORE PATRONAGE BEHAVIOR
A study of the interface between retailers and consumers

By

TORBEN HANSEN
Copenhagen Business School

and

HANS STUBBE SOLGAARD
Copenhagen Business School

Kluwer Academic Publishers
Boston, New York, Dordrecht

Distributors for North, Central and South America:
Kluwer Academic Publishers
101 Philip Drive
Assinippi Park
Norwell, Massachusetts 02061 USA
Telephone (781) 871-6600
Fax (781) 681-9045
E-Mail <kluwer@wkap.com>
Distributors for all other countries:
Kluwer Academic Publishers Group
Post Office Box 17
3300 AH Dordrecht, THE NETHERLANDS
Tel: +31 (0) 78 657 60 00
Fax: +31 (0) 78 657 64 74

E-Mail <services@wkap.nl>

 Electronic Services <http://www.wkap.nl>

New Perspectives on Retailing and Store Patronage Behavior:
 A Study of the Interface Between Retailers and Consumers
 By Torben Hansen and Hans Stubbe Solgaard
         p.cm.
  Includes bibliographical references and index.
  ISBN 1-4020-7954-0 (alk.paper)
  E-ISBN 1-4020-7955-9

Permission for books published in Europe: permissions@wkap.nl
Permissions for books published in the United States of America: permissions@wkap.com
Printed on acid-free paper.
Printed in the United States of America

***The Publisher offers discounts on this book for course use and bulk purchases.
For further information, send email to <kluwer@wkap.com>.***

Preface

Retailing and consumer patronage behavior constitute fascinating research areas within the field of marketing. Retailing contributes to an increasing proportion of gross national products and employment but is, however, also faced with problems and opportunities like increased product complexity, rapidly changing consumer expectations, and the introduction of new technologies. Also, consumers are facing markets of increasingly complexity when making decisions on how to conduct their behavior, primarily as a result of new technologies, shorter products life cycles in general, and higher complexity of products and services.

In this book, we present and deal with various topics in relation to retailing and consumer patronage behavior. Together, these topics involve different problem settings and draw on different theories, models and statistical techniques. However, it is common to all the results presented in the following chapters (with the exception of chapter II) that they, in total or in part, rest on a major survey, which was conducted by the authors in 1999. Our now retired colleague, Hans Engstrøm participated in preparing this survey and did a great job in providing research ideas. For this, and for many stimulating discussions, we are highly grateful.

The details of the survey is outlined in chapter I. Minor descriptions of the survey design may also be found in the individual chapters, which constitute the body of this book. We have chosen this method of presentation to allow readers interested in just one or few of the chapters to focus on these without having to read the introductory chapter or other chapters.

The major purpose of the present book has not been to write a 'textbook'. Excellent textbooks covering the many facets of retailing and consumer patronage behavior do already exist. Instead, our main purpose has been to provide an in-depth investigation and discussion of some selected topics, which in our opinion are among the more interesting and evolving contemporary topics within the field of retailing and consumer patronage behavior.

Copenhagen, 2004.

Torben Hansen and Hans Stubbe Solgaard.

Contents

CHAPTER VI
INTERTYPE COMPETITION

CHAPTER VII
EPILOGUE

Chapter 1

INTRODUCTION

1.   BACKGROUND AND OBJECTIVES

This book is about consumers and retailers, and the relations between them. Retailing constitutes an important part of the private service sector in all countries of the European Union, and contributes to an increasing proportion of gross national products and employment. Retailers form together with wholesalers the vital links between the various actors in the national economies, i.e. agriculture, industry, the service sector, the public sector and the private households. Retailing comes at the very end of the supply chain, and provides the final link to the households or consumers, hence retailing in general plays an important role in the every-day-life of most people. Therefore, it is not surprising that retailing often is on the public and political agenda in many countries, and a lot of knowledge about the sector has accumulated. Generally, however, the debate concerns regulation of the sector, such as imposing constraints on opening hours, establishing rules for center planning, evaluating the structural development of the sector, and taxation, whereas there is only little publicly available and applicable statistics and other information to shed light on consumers' perceptions, attitudes and behaviors towards retailers.

Retailers and consumers impinge on each other. Retailers influence consumers in the short run through their ongoing marketing activities, and in the longer run the challenges facing retailers in the form of new technology, emerging electronic markets, increasing concentration, erosion of sector barriers and so on, also will have some bearing on consumers and buying behavior. Likewise consumers constantly influence retailers through changing preferences and expectations. Given the paucity of empirical knowledge concerning the relations between retailers and consumers, there is a need at suitable intervals for data and information concerning consumer perceptions, attitudes and behaviors towards retailers.

Against this background it is the objective of this book to present contemporary perspectives on the relations between consumers and retailers, and in addition to present and explore the usefulness of modern quantitative techniques, such as linear structural relationships modeling (LISREL), hierarchical Bayes modeling, and correspondence analysis. Specifically we investigate how consumers, retailers and producers perceive the concept of food product quality. We analyze consumers' perceptions of grocery retail store chains, and identify and scrutinize the determinant factors in consumers' store choice between different grocery store formats. Finally, we probe into the competition between specialty food stores and supermarkets. The research is performed in a Danish setting

In the following we describe the setting for this research, the grocery retail market in Denmark, and outline the survey design used to collect the data. We conclude this introduction with an overview of chapters.

2. THE RESEARCH SETTING

Developments in Danish retailing, and in particular in Danish grocery retailing, over the last 20+ years have followed the general European trends. A sharp decline in the number of grocery retail stores complemented by a larger geographical and economical concentration has taken place. Additionally the emergence of discount grocery store chains, and a strong increase in the number of discount outlets over the years has been observed. Moreover, quite similar to the developments in most Western countries, the diffusion of information technology throughout the Danish grocery sector has had an important impact, in particular, on the relation between retailers and suppliers/producers and in more recent years also on the relation between retailers and consumers. Although parallel processes of structural change are evident across Europe there are substantial differences between the different countries and regions of Europe. In the following we briefly look at these trends and the placement of Denmark within these trends.

Looking first at the process of concentration and internationalization this process did not start until the late eighties, and first really took off when the Single European market came into effect in 1992. By 1989 the top ten European retailers accounted for less than 20% of food and grocery sales, this increased to 27% by 1992 and further to 36% in 1997, Dawson (1999), M+M Eurodata (1999), and is forecasted to grow to about 70% within the next 10 years, (EMD, 2003). This concentration has meant a sharp reduction in the number of retailers across Europe and an internationalization of retailing in Europe, and has created fear for reduction of competition in the retail sector. The level of concentration and internationalization varies, however, widely across Europe. Thus there is a clear North-South divide among European countries in terms of concentration. Most of the national food retail markets in North-Western Europe (Scandinavia, Germany, the UK, Benelux and France) are highly concentrated with the top five retailers accounting for market shares in the range of 60% to 75%. In Denmark the top two retailers alone have a market share of around 68%. The national markets in Southern Europe, (Italy, Greece and Spain), however, are much more fragmented with the top five retailers having market shares in the range of 20% to 45%, (Wrigley, 2002).

Considering the internationalization of retailing this process has primarily been driven by French and Dutch companies, and to a lesser degree by German, Belgian and British firms. The number of international hyper- and supermarkets in these countries are naturally low being in the range of 1% to 3% of the total number of hyper- and supermarkets, with Germany being the exception with 13%. Countries on the receiving end of internationalization are primarily the countries of Southern Europe, Italy, Spain and Portugal, and East European countries, such as the Czech Republic and Poland, Poole et al. (2002) also refer to Wrigley (2002). The process of internationalization has also reached Denmark, thus the discount grocery chain Netto owned by the second largest retailer Dansk Supermarked Ltd. has expanded into three foreign markets and plans to further expand. Furthermore the largest retailer FDB a consumer co-operative has in 2001 merged with its cooperative sister companies in Sweden and Norway, and formed COOP Nordic in order to be able to take up a potential challenge from foreign retailers. Aldi the German discount chain has operated in Denmark in the last 15 years and has a market share of around 4% of the grocery market. Other foreign retailers are present on the Danish market albeit at a small scale, thus the Dutch giant Ahold owns the Danish supermarket chain ISO via the Swedish retailer ICA.

Regarding discount food retailing this business format was in 2000 present in all European countries with 29.747 stores and with an overall market share of 15% of food sales. Market shares varies, however, significantly among the countries from 4.2% in Greece to 42.9% in Norway, see Table 1. A clear North-South divide appears from Table 1 with small market shares in the Southern countries and high shares in the Northern countries. From 1995 to 2000 discount retailers experienced slow growth in terms of market shares, however, it has increased in the majority of the countries exceptions being the UK, Italy and Switzerland, Colla (2003). In Denmark discount retailers have penetrated the market over the last 15 to 20 years and obtained a considerable share of the market. Thus discount retailers in 1991 accounted for 15% of grocery sales, in 1995 for 20% and in 2000 for 23% of sales, this share is forecasted to grow to 28% in 2006, Stockmann Group (2001), (2002).

Table 1 Market share of discount food retailing 1995-2000 in Europe

Country	Market share 1995	Market share 2000
Norway	38.3	42.9
Germany	29.5	32.6
Belgium	24.7	27.8
Denmark	20.0	23.0
Austria	16.5	21.8
Sweden	11.0	15.2
The Netherlands	12.2	14.1
Finland	10.7	11.2
Spain	6.5	9.5
Portugal	6.1	9.5
United Kingdom	11.3	8.2
France	6.4	7.9
Switzerland	8.6	7.9
Italy	9.7	6.7
Greece	1.6	4.2
Total	13.6	14.9

Source: A.C. Nielsen in Colla (2003)

2.1   The Danish retail structure

The Danish grocery retail market can be partitioned into six strategic groups each offering a unique mix of price, service and assortments. Three of these strategic groups, hypermarkets, discount supermarkets and conventional supermarkets, compete for major shopping trips of consumers and may be denoted the 'supermarket market' (Marion, 1998). The remaining three groups, mini-markets, specialty food stores, and kiosks, compete for fill-in or specialty shopping, and this market may be labeled the 'fill-in market', (Marion, 1998). In this book we primarily consider the supermarket market, and to a lesser degree the fill-in market, where focus will be on specialty stores.

Various formats constitute the supermarket market in Denmark, namely discount stores, hypermarkets, and conventional supermarkets (including up-scale supermarkets). Two large supermarket groups, Dansk Supermarked and Coop Nordic (formerly FDB), dominate the Danish supermarket market having a total market share of 68% (2000). The corporate retail chain Dansk Supermarked (market share 25%) is owned by Dansk Supermarked Ltd, whereas Coop Nordic (market share 43%) is a consumer co-op. The Danish independents hold together 28% of the market. Of the independents 55% are joined in wholesale-sponsored voluntary cooperative groups, whereas 32% are joined in retail-sponsored cooperatives. Aldi the German discount store chain holds a market share of 4% of the supermarket market. Dansk Supermarked comprises the discount store chain Netto (market share 10%), the hypermarket chain BILKA (market share 5%), and the combination store/conventional supermarket chain FØTEX (market share 10%). Coop Nordic comprises the discount store chain Fakta (market share 10%), the hypermarket chain OBS (market share 3%), the combination store/conventional supermarket chain Kvickly (market share 9%), the conventional supermarket chains SuperBrugsen (market share 16%) and Dagli'Brugsen (market share 5%), and the up-scale conventional supermarket chain IRMA (market share 2%). The Danish independents, among them the up-scale chain ISO, comprise conventional supermarkets (total market share 22%), discount supermarkets (total market share 4%) and others (market share 2%).

Danish specialty stores can be characterized as owner managed independents. Cooperation and integration among these stores is almost absent, (Stockmann Group, 2000). In 2000 there were a total of 5700 specialty stores in Denmark with a market share in the fill in market of about 45%.

3. THE DATA.

The input for this research is provided by data from a survey of grocery shopping conducted in the greater Copenhagen metropolitan area in the spring of 1999 by the authors. The retail structure in this area is well described by the structure of the supermarket market in Denmark. The target population consisted of households, and in order to draw a balanced proportion of respondents we applied stratified sampling. As stratification variables we used personal income and dwelling type. The reasons for this are the following observations. First a survey of personal incomes in the population revealed considerable variation in the average personal income across the fifty municipalities constituting the metropolitan area. Since personal income is an important factor in the planning of buying behavior for most households, and in addition easily accessible in public statistics we decided to use the fifty municipalities as strata to secure that all income groups would be represented as accurate as possible in the sample. Second, strong differences with respect to type of dwelling can be observed across the fifty municipalities, thus in the Copenhagen municipality 88.4% of all dwellings are apartment houses and only 11.6 % one family houses, whereas the opposite is the case in some of the more distant (from the city of

Copenhagen) municipalities. Since type of dwelling may reflect differences in life style that may influence buying behavior, we decided to partition each stratum into two substrata according to the proportions of the dwelling types. In each stratum a sample proportionate to the relative size of that stratum in the total population was selected, and in each stratum households were sampled among dwelling types according to the relative number of the two types of dwellings in the stratum. Respondents were selected using systematic random sampling.

In all 1500 households were contacted and 631 responded with useable questionnaires resulting in a response rate of 42%. The questionnaires were distributed to the respondents using the 'drop-off-call-back' method (Haire et al. 1998), with the help from 58 graduate students in business administration, who were instructed to serve as data collectors. The respondents were approached in their home, and if a respondent agreed to participate in the study, the student made an appointment to return for the completed questionnaire. When picking up the questionnaire the student made sure that it was correctly completed, and provided answers to questions and comments that the respondent might have. The person in the household most often responsible for the grocery shopping was chosen as the respondent.

The variables included in the questionnaire can be partitioned into four sets,

a) Variables describing to the buying pattern of the household.
b) Variables measuring the household's perception and evaluation of store chains.
c) Variables describing the household.
d) Variables pertaining to household's behavior towards and perception of specialty stores.

A detailed description of the variables selected and utilized for the empirical analyses will be given in the individual chapters, which constitute the book.

4. THE CONTENT

In *chapter II* we explore the potential problem that different agents in the marketplace may attach different meanings to various concepts. This may especially be the case for concepts, which are ambiguous in nature, i.e. concepts for which no commonly agreed definition or conceptualization seems to exist. Quality is such an ambiguous concept. Though a number of authors have contributed with both classifications and definitions there is still considerable confusion about the application of quality. In chapter II, quality is seen in the context of the essential transformation problem, which may exist between the supplier and the customer. On this basis, a common frame of reference for dealing with the concept of quality is proposed. It is further underlined that it is vital for a successful implementation of TQM for there to be a correspondence between the suppliers' and their customers' interpretations of quality. Empirical evidence indicates, however, that suppliers (food producers and food retailers) may use the concept of quality in an inconsistent way when dealing with the concept in the marketplace.

In *chapter III* we investigate the image and positions of eleven grocery store chains that are rated in our survey of buying behavior. To evaluate consumer perceptions of the grocery chains we employ correspondence analysis and in order to take the nature of the consumer ratings into account we apply correspondence analysis. To complement the results of the correspondence analysis we perform a cluster analysis. The picture that emerges from these analyses generally indicates that consumers' perceptions are consistent with the store chains' desired image position as discount stores, hypermarkets or conventional supermarkets. The discount stores, thus indeed are perceived as stores offering low prices and good specials, but they are also being rated very low on all other image aspects. In spite of this the discount chains have over the last 10 to 15 years gained a considerable market share of the grocery retail sector, indicating that the perceived price gaps between the various store formats in the supermarket market still are sufficiently large to be a major driver of consumer's decision of where to shop.

In *chapter IV* we probe further into the drivers of the decision of where to shop. We develop and estimate a model of consumer's choice between different supermarket formats. Three formats are considered, conventional supermarkets, characterized in general terms by high-low pricing, broad and deep assortments and some service, discount stores characterized by everyday-low-pricing, narrow assortments, and no service, and hypermarkets, characterized by a pricing policy somewhat in between the two other formats, wide and deep assortments, and low service. Our model is developed within the framework of the multinomial logit model that has been widely used in retailing but also strongly criticized. We discuss the problems involved in operationalizing the model using this framework and suggest a random coefficients logit model to remedy these problems. We estimate the model as a hierarchical Bayes model, and assess the importance of the choice determinants by analyzing direct- and cross choice elasticities. The results indicate that distance (location), assortment and price level are the most important variables, but also that there are a substantial amount of heterogeneity among consumers in sensitivities to price level and assortment, and in particular to distance.

We take a further look at the influence of the distance variable in store choice in *chapter V*. We propose that the significance of distance is influenced by the way in which store choice behavior is construed. Considering distance in a value perspective we develop a conceptual model of store choice, where the store choice decision is specified as a function of the perceived value of the service outputs offered by a store and the perceived costs related to 'price-level' and 'distance'. The model is translated into a LISREL model, and the structural equation results suggest that the negative effect of distance on store choice behavior is larger when store choice behavior is measured as number of visits to a particular store than when store choice behavior is measured as the percentage of budget spend at a particular store.

Empirical findings are presented in *chapter VI* concerning the competitiveness of specialty food stores when competing with supermarkets. An analysis of the Danish food retail market shows that some remarkable changes have taken place: (1) A dramatic closure of specialty food shops, (2) a dramatic decrease in the market share obtained by specialty food stores, (3) a steady rise in the average grocery store size, (4) a successful introduction of discount supermarkets, (5) a higher economic and geographic concentration level, and (6) both supermarkets and the remaining specialty food stores have managed to increase their gross profit ratio. Taking both a specialty food store-oriented perspective and a consumer-oriented perspective, empirical evidence suggests that specialty food store managers' and consumers' evaluation of the importance of various store choice factors are quite similar. However, the results also indicate the presence of a 'gap' between consumer and specialty food store managers regarding the assortment factor. While managers see assortment as a relatively unimportant factor consumers regard assortment as a very important factor for their store choice behavior. It is therefore suggested that specialty food store managers should adjust their in-store assortment in order to reduce the 'assortment-gab' and thereby reduce the risk that consumers become unsatisfied. In general, specialty food store managers show, however, highly positive expectations towards future intertype competition with supermarkets.

In the concluding *chapter VII* we consider a number of additional topics, which we believe will receive increasingly importance and consideration by researchers and retail management. In relation to each topic we provide suggestions for future research.

REFERENCES

Colla, E. (2003), "International expansion and strategies of discount grocery retailers: the winning models", *International Journal of Retail & Distribution Management*, vol. 31, no. 1, pp. 55-66.

Dawson, J. A. (1999), "Employment and Competitiveness in European Commerce", *Commerce 99: Seminar on Distributive Trades in Europe*, Eurostat and Enterprise DG, Brussels 22-23 November.

EMD (2003), www.emd-ag.com/e/markt002.shtm, EMD AG, Pfäffikon.

Hair, J.F, R.E. Anderson, R.L. Tatham and W.C. Black (1998), *Multivariate Data Analysis*, Fifth ed, Prentice-Hall International, NJ.

M+M Eurodata (1999), *Top Firmen*, M+M Frankfurt am Main.

Marion, B.W. (1998), Competition in Grocery Retailing: The Impact of a New Strategic Group on BLS Price Increases. *Review of Industrial Organization*, vol.13, pp. 381-99.

Poole, R., Clarke, G.P. and Clarke, D.B. (2002), "Growth, Concentration and Regulation in European Food Retailing", *European Urban and Regional Studies*, vol. 9, no. 2, pp. 167-186.

Stockmann Group (2001), *Dansk Dagligvarehandel, 10 Årsstatistik 1991-2000.*

Stockmann Group (2001), *Supermarkedshåndbogen* 2000

Stockmann Group (2002), *Supermarkedshåndbogen* 2003.

Wrigley, N. (2002), "The Landscape of pan-European food retail consolidation", *International Journal of Retail & Distribution Management*, vol. 30, no. 2, pp. 81-91.

Chapter 2

QUALITY IN THE MARKETPLACE·
a theoretical and empirical investigation

1.   INTRODUCTION

It seems to be a well-established fact that leaders, economical actors and others to a certain degree act and use concepts, because these concepts and acts are in fashion (Abrahamson, 1996). This thought is recognized in 'institutionalization theory', which assumes the presence of an isomorfistic pattern of development in businesses (Scott & Meyer, 1994), just as the empirically based literature contains many examples of 'fashion' as a decision variable (see e.g. Rumelt, 1974; Mintzberg, 1979; Kobrin, 1988). 'Quality' is certainly among the concepts that are in fashion (see e.g. Neergaard, 1998) and that to a large extent can be used by researchers and practitioners alike as a basis for analyses in relation to business competitiveness, business image, customer loyalty etc. However, the interest in the concept of quality is not incidental. On the contrary, there are countless examples of quality as a key factor in the competition between businesses. After having completed 1135 personal interviews with small and medium-sized companies, Bamberger (1989) arrived at the conclusion that out of a total of 26 parameters quality is viewed as the most important parameter in creating a competitive edge. Porter (1980) emphasizes that aiming for (superior) quality could be an effective competitive strategy in developing customer loyalty, lowering price elasticity or barring other

· Reprinted from European Management Journal, Vol. 19, No. 2, Hansen, Torben, Quality in the Marketplace: A Theoretical and Empirical Investigation, pp. 203-211, Copyright (2001), with permission from Elsevier Science.

potential competitors from entering the market. The implementation of quality strategies could create a higher rate of profit (Johnson & Kleiner, 1993), as well as greater market shares (Jacobson & Aaker, 1987; Curry & Riesz, 1988). Kirkpatrick and Locke (1996) point out that "quality…reflects the vision of modern companies" (p. 37).

Nevertheless, researchers far from agree on the meaning of the concept of quality in the literature. Many authors, e.g. Neergaard (1998), Grunert et al. (1996), Reeves and Bednar (1994), Steenkamp (1989), Garvin (1984) and Holbrook and Corfman (1985), have attempted to provide an overview of 'the quality theory'. However, among these and other authors, there are divergent notions of the concept of quality regarding the number as well as the description of the various interpretations of the concept. Unfortunately, the conceptual confusion within the theoretical literature is a major hindrance for obtaining wider recognition. The damage is even worse when the concept of quality is part of a current fashion within the world of management, research and consulting, as is the case. The number of potential misunderstandings and lapses in communication thus seems uncountable. In this article, we will be mapping different theoretical and practical interpretations of quality. We will be uniting them under a common frame of reference, as well as demonstrating that in practice (which in the present context will be restricted to encompass the relation between producers and consumers and the relation between retailers and consumers) the use of the concept of quality seems to be somewhat inconsistent, even coincidental.

2.   THE CONCEPT OF QUALITY

A great part of modern literature on quality deals with the philosophy of Total Quality Management (TQM) (Dale et al., 1994; Neergaard, 1998). TQM does not in itself represent a model or a technique, but is best described as a management philosophy cf. Snell & Dean's (1992) definition: "TQM…is characterized by a few basic principles – doing things right the first time, striving for continuous improvement, and fulfilling consumer needs – as well as a number of associated practices" (p. 470). However, attempts at establishing general guidelines for the use of TQM have been made. These include attempts initiated in connection with the European Quality Award (developed by the European Foundation for Quality Management, which was founded in 1989 by a number of European Companies) (see e.g. Neergaard, 1998 for an in depth description). According to Nilsson (1998), the goal for TQM is "to achieve competitive advantage within all areas of the company, based on a set of fairly general principles of motivation and learning, and organization theory" (p. 40). These principles have also been described as 'the three TQM principles': customer focus, continuous improvement, and teamwork (Goetsch & Davis, 1994; Dean & Bowen, 1994; Parzinger & Nath, 2000).

The implementation of a 'quality management philosophy' in the company is, however, contingent upon the company clearly conceptualizing their notion of quality. This was done by e.g. Oakland (1993): "Quality then, is simply meeting the customer requirements and this has been expressed in many ways by other authors" (p. 5). However, quality perceived as the fulfilled requirements of the customer only represents one out of several alternative interpretations of the concept of quality. The company will thus have to consider these alternative interpretations when formulating their TQM strategy. They should also aim to have an understanding of the different notions of quality. Regardless of whether the company makes use of different concepts of quality internally (e.g., the interpretation of quality can vary depending on whether the question is human resource management or quality control), they will, of course, be faced with having to present their products on the market at some point in time. In this connection, it is vital for the successful implementation of TQM that the company has considered the following: (a) how they would assess the market quality of their products themselves (i.e., how the company perceives the concept of quality in the marketplace). (b) How their customers assess the market quality (i.e., how the company's customers perceive the concept of quality in the marketplace). And finally, (c) that the company and their customers' interpretation of quality correspond. An inconsistency between the company and their customers' interpretation of quality could easily lead to the two parties 'passing each other by' in the marketplace. For example, it is very difficult for a company to try to improve the quality of their products, if their customers' interpretation of what quality is differs from their own.

In general, quality can, on the one hand, be viewed from the producer's side (producer's criteria) and, on the other hand, from the consumer's side (consumer's criteria). Producer's criteria are "criteria which describe what the producer put into the product" and consumer's criteria are "criteria which describe what the consumer gets from the product" (Brems, 1951, pp. 18-19). At the same time, consumer's criteria describe what the consumer wants from the product. Five general interpretations of the concept of quality, emerging from an extensive analysis of the literature about quality, will be discussed in the following. The five interpretations of quality may be combined in a common frame of reference as proposed in Figure 1[1]. The Figure will be commented on further in the following.

---

1 The composition of the frame of reference owes some inspiration to Steenkamp (1989, p. 96).

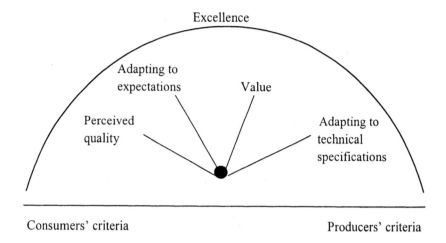

Figure 1. Alternative interpretations of quality

2.1   The consumer's perception of quality

Perceived quality is a result of the consumer's (the buyer's) subjective assessment of the quality of a given product. Perceived quality thus differs from objective quality. Objective quality may be described as "the measurable and verifiable superiority on some predetermined ideal standards" (Zeithaml, 1988, p. 4). Objective quality can thus be construed as the technical and functional specifications of a product. Subjective quality on the other hand is linked to the consumer and her/his perception of the quality of a product. Quality is thus individually determined and consequently, it can hardly be generally determined for all consumers and thus you end up with a problem of generalization. Literature about quality has shown that the individual perception of quality is influenced by a number of factors (e.g. prior experience, purpose of use, quality consciousness etc.) (see e.g. Steenkamp, 1989; Peterson & Jolibert, 1995; Dodds, 1995) that either relate to the consumer her/himself or to external factors. The dimensions of the product that influence the perception of quality are dependent on the given product (Aaker, 1991; Dodds et al., 1991; Bauer et al., 1995). The consumer's perception of quality may, in other words, be seen as an expression of her/his own interpretation of the concept of quality and accordingly, it has been placed to the left of Figure 1 under the heading 'consumer's criteria'.

2.2   Quality as adaptation to expectations

In the literature about quality, the so-called 'quality gap' is discussed; this gap appears when there is an inconsistency between the expectation of quality and the perception of quality (Zeithaml et al., 1990; Devling & Dong, 1994). Bergman and Klefsjö (1994, p. 282), correspondingly, define the quality of a product as "its ability to satisfy the expectations and needs of the customers". Satisfaction, thus, becomes a parameter for measuring whether and to what degree the customers' expectations have been met. It is difficult, however, to determine when all the customers' expectations have been met as it seems possible to exceed their expectations (Rust & Oliver, 1994), for example when companies 'keep more than their promise'. Furthermore, sometimes the customer does not initially know what her/his specific expectations are. After having consumed a food product, the consumer may conclude that her/his expectations were not quite met without being able to specify what her/his expectations were (Reeves & Bednar, 1994). Using this interpretation, one will also typically be faced with a problem of generalization, as it is impossible to develop a unique product for each individual consumer. The problem of generalization can often be solved by developing a product of as high an 'objective quality' as possible, thus assuming that such a product will be able to satisfy the most consumers (Gavin, 1984). Finally, it also constitutes a problem, if the customer's satisfaction is based on low initial expectations of the product. This does not actually mean that the consumer perceives the product to be of high quality. E.g., if you buy a large cheese for $ 1,00 from a discount store, you would hardly expect very much in the way of quality. Even if your assessment turns out to be correct and your initial low expectations are thus met (and you are 'satisfied'), it does not necessarily follow that you will think that it is a high quality product. Quality as 'adaptation to expectations' is based on the consumer's own assessment of quality, but also include the producer's criteria via the expectations that they seek to market with their product or service. Therefore, 'quality as adaptation to expectations' has been placed slightly to the right of the 'perceived quality' of the consumer.

2.3   Quality as value

The concept of value has a prominent position in the classic micro-economical tradition. The notion that the quality of a product should be determined in relation to its price and not solely by its own merits is comprised in this concept. The relation between price and quality thus determines the value of the product. As well as finding use within economical theory, the concept of value is used in literature about behavior, psychology and sociology, although it often refers to a more 'abstract' value here, such as 'personal value' and 'symbolic value'. According to Abbott (1955, p. 108), both price and quality should be given due consideration when a company wants to enter a competitive market. : "how good a bargain anything is depends upon both quality and price; the two elements compounded together form the basis for evaluation of winning contestants in the market place. Only when differences in quality have been eliminated by standardisation does 'cheapest' necessarily coincide with best."

According to Curry (1985), consumers clearly acknowledge the differences in value of various products, which (according to Curry) can be inferred from the fact that companies that offer quality products at low prices typically dominate the market. The concept of value, therefore, encourages the companies to focus on internal economic efficiency (low cost), as well as external efficiency (the satisfaction of consumers' wants and needs). By determining the value of a product, instead of looking at price or quality separately, it will be possible to immediately compare the value of the various products and thereby also their ability to satisfy the consumer. However, this would presuppose a common notion among consumers of what is good and bad quality as well as high and low prices. Thus, some standard of objective quality that all consumers agree on must be reached. Even if it were possible to objectively measure quality or quality characteristics (as for example Lancaster's (1966, 1971) consumer theory presupposes) different consumers' preferences for those objective qualities may still vary. For this reason, it is difficult to make any general statements about which products satisfy the consumer most, even when using an objective concept of value. Furthermore, one may very well question whether consumers even perceive quality (and price) and thus value alike. If we assume that they do not, it becomes more interesting to examine *perceived* value and subsequently *perceived* quality, i.e., what the consumer perceives as quality. Moreover, separating quality and price involves a risk of misinterpretation since the consumer may choose to perceive the quality of a product as higher as a result of a higher price (see e.g., Leavitt, 1954; Steenkamp, 1989; Dodds, 1995)! In this case, the value would remain the same, even though it should have plummeted (as a result of a negative change in price and no change in quality). The interpretation of value comprises both producer and consumer perspectives, and has thus been placed close to the middle of Figure 1. However, the producer's view seems to be more predominant in this particular interpretation, i.e., there is a tendency to view the world from the perspective of the producer.

2.4 Quality as adaptation to technical specifications

In this interpretation, quality is viewed as an objective, measurable variable, which can be described in terms of technical specifications. The better the product meets these specifications, the better the quality. Any deviations would mean depreciation in quality. This is a well-known phenomenon in 'quality control'; see e.g. Bergman and Kelfsjö (1994). Quality as adaptation to technical specifications expresses the basic criteria of the producer and has thus been placed to the right of Figure 1 under the heading 'producer's criteria'.

2.5 Quality as excellence

On more than one occasion, quality has been described as an expression of excellence (see e.g. Pirsig, 1974; Garvin, 1984; Tuchman, 1980; Reeves & Bednar, 1994). Products of high quality thus become the 'best' products, i.e., those products that meet the highest standards. However, it could prove difficult to determine the precise quality of products that do not quite meet these standards. Conversely, it is easy to determine what products are not quality products, i.e., those products that are 'inferior' according to the set standards. The problem is a question of who should set the standards; should the standards be set from the producer, the consumer or society's points of view? Can a satisfactory scale even be established? The concept of excellence is part of the campaign foundation for auto makers such as 'Mercedes', 'BMW' and 'Cadillac'; spirit makers such as 'Chivas Regal' and 'Crown Royal'; and finally, airlines such as 'Singapore Airlines' and 'British Air' (Reeves & Bednar, 1994). Consumers that buy these businesses' products and services are promised that they will be envied by other consumers, who have made less sensible choices. The auto maker, 'Chrysler' seems to follow the concept of excellence suit with the following advertisement caption: "At Chrysler we have only one ambition. To be the best. What else is there?" (Caption borrowed from Assael, 1995, p. 723). The concept of excellence dates back to the Greek philosophers, primarily Socrates, Plato and Aristotle who promoted the ideal of excellence for the Greeks (Reeves & Bednar, 1994). In ancient Greece, excellence referred to 'the highest form', 'the best' and 'the highest idea'. Dating back to Greek philosophy, 'quality as excellence' is probably the most abstract of the five interpretations; it may include the others, albeit without specifically subscribing to any of them. Reaching excellence may be set as a general goal for the business, regardless of their specific interpretation of quality. Thus, quality as excellence is seen as a general interpretation in Figure 1.

To provide a more detailed description of the five interpretations of quality, the relations between producer's and consumer's criteria may be presented as follows (Rørsted, 1970):

The producer's criteria are given by:

$$\alpha 1,\ \alpha 2,\ \alpha 3,\ ...\alpha n$$

The consumer's criteria are then given by:

$$\beta 1,\ \beta 2,\ \beta 3,...\beta n$$

The sale of the produced products may be formulated as a function of the consumer's criteria, so that:

$$qd = q(p,\ \beta 1,\ \beta 2,..\beta n) \quad (1)$$

The criteria concern all of the characteristics of the products that are in demand by the consumers for a price or are offered to the consumers for a price, i.e., quality and price. The demand for quality is thus made up of a certain combination of consumer criteria for a set price. The following functional relation between producer and consumer criteria may now be formulated:

$$\alpha i = \alpha i\ (\beta 1,\ \beta 2,..\beta n) \quad (2)$$

$$\beta j = \beta j\ (\alpha 1,\ \alpha 2,...\alpha n) \quad (3)$$

(2) shows that the interpretations of quality placed under producer's criteria in Figure 1 are influenced by the interpretations of quality placed under consumer's criteria. That is, the consumer criteria must be transformed into producer criteria. If consumer and producer criteria are in accordance, and consumer and producer also agree on a common interpretation of quality, the above-mentioned relation presents no problems. However, where significant discordance between the two types of criteria or between consumer and producer's interpretations of quality exist, the transformation from consumer to producer criteria may prove more difficult. (3) tells us that the interpretations of quality placed under consumer's criteria in Figure 1 are influenced by the interpretations placed under producer's criteria. This can best be explained by the fact that the quality features the producer supplies, e.g., technical features, must necessarily be transformed to the consumer's criteria in order for them to have an utility value. In (1), price is seen as a separate variable. As far as price is concerned, this is due to the fact that any

transformation problems are considered less significant since price must be viewed as relatively objective from the consumer and producers' points of view.

The placing of the individual interpretations in relation to each other, as suggested in Figure 1, presents a number of problems in itself. Figure 1 points towards the very significant transformation problem, which might occur between producer and consumer. If the quality features, which the producer supplies with the product, are not in accordance with the quality features the consumer ascribes to the product, the transformation could prove very difficult. The consumer does not evaluate objective qualities, s/he evaluates attributes (i.e., 'ascribed qualities'), and the two are not necessarily in accordance. In other words, the producer must 'translate' consumer criteria to producer criteria before the drafting of the product, and subsequently, the producer must translate these criteria to 'consumer language'. In this connection, it is evident that any disagreement between producer and consumer regarding how quality should be assessed when products are being marketed, could make the transformation process considerably more difficult, and thus also inhibit the establishment of an effective quality management philosophy in the company. This does not prevent the company from operating with several interpretations of quality, e.g., the production process may depend on the fulfillment of a number of cited technical specifications, while the marketing of the finished products on the market may take as its point of departure 'to fulfill the expectations of the consumers', or to create the best 'value', or to offer 'excellent products', or to offer certain 'technical specifications'. For the transformation process to be a success, it is, however, necessary that the companies and the consumer in the market place share a common perception of what quality is, regardless of the company's internal use of the concept of quality. Two empirical analyses were carried out to examine the practical meaning and extension of this problem. These will be outlined in the following.

3. METHOD

The realization of a fragmentation of the theoretical concept of quality, which we have emphasized in the above, is the point of departure for the following studies. Two studies were carried out to examine the problem in question.

3.1   Study 1

The first study was conducted as a mail survey among Danish food producers from all parts of the country. The managers of the companies were asked to rank the five outlined interpretations of quality: first according to which interpretations of quality they themselves believe to be the most correct when competing on the market; and second according to what interpretations of quality they think the consumers believe to be the most correct when they interact with the market. To limit any uncertainty about interpretations of quality determined by the product, we chose to limit ourselves to the food industry. A total of 49 randomly chosen executive managers in the foods industry got a questionnaire in the mail. 43% of the participating managers returned the questionnaire; among these one manager did not wish to participate, while two companies had ceased to exist, which meant that a total of 19 companies participated in study 1. The respondents were guaranteed confidentiality and were instructed to return the questionnaires to the university, where the study was being conducted. A self-addressed, stamped envelope was enclosed in the letter.

3.2   Study 2

This study was also conducted as a mail survey. The study consists of 163 specialty food store managers from all parts of Denmark. 960 survey questionnaires were distributed for this study, resulting in a response rate of 17.0%. The managers were asked the same questions as in study 1, and were once again guaranteed full confidentiality and provided with a self-addressed, stamped envelope.

4.   THE OPERATIONALIZATION OF THE FIVE INTERPRETATIONS OF QUALITY

Firstly, it was very important that the theoretical concepts (the interpretations of quality) and the operationalization of the interpretations of quality that were used were in accordance. Secondly, it was of great importance that the operationalizations were perceived by the respondents as intended. The following procedures were used in order to ensure the above (Bagozzi, 1994):

A preliminary first draft based on already existing theoretical and empirical studies was prepared for the operationalization of the theoretical concepts.

Four researchers particularly competent in the quality area, and who had been briefed regarding the design and purpose of the study subsequently assessed the draft. Five non-experts also assessed the draft. The purpose of this was to avoid any inaccuracies and ambiguities in the questions and thus get a first impression of the validity of the operationalizations. This step resulted in a number of adjustments in the operationalizations.

Following these adjustments, the questions were shown to two more experts and three non-experts. This step resulted in minor corrections only.

Finally, a pre-test was carried out (n=10, non-experts). This test did not result in any further adjustments of the operationalizations used.

5. RESULTS

In one of the questions, the companies were asked to rank the five mentioned interpretations of quality based on what the companies themselves regard as most correct for use in the marketplace:

Table 1 shows that the preferred interpretation of quality of both the food producers and the specialty food stores is 'quality as adaptation to expectations'. There is, however, some disagreement between the two groups of respondents as the food producers rank 'quality as excellence' as no. 5, whereas the specialty food stores rank this interpretation as no. 2. This difference of opinion is probably due to the fact that the specialty food stores traditionally offer quality and professional service, whereas the foods producers together represent a mélange of low quality and high quality producers.

Table 1. The companies' perception of quality

Interpretations of quality	Study 1		Study 2	
	Total#	Rank	Total#	Rank
Quality as an excellent product	71	5	392	2
Quality as value	50	2	560	4
Quality as the consumers perceive it	59	4	502	3
Quality as adaptation to expectations	35	1	316	1
Quality as adaptation to technical specifications	55	3	675	5

The lowest value indicates the most preferred interpretation of quality

The ranking of 'quality as adaptation to expectations' as no. 1 would indicate that, according to the companies, food products can be good quality products, even if they do not live up to the highest standards in the market, as long as the consumers perceive the products as the same every time: If the products appear the same every time, consumers with prior knowledge of products will be able to form realistic expectations of the quality more easily. Consequently, consumers will feel that their expectations are being fulfilled to a larger degree. Table 1 also shows that the producers rank 'quality as adaptation to technical specifications' as no. 3, while the specialty food stores rank this interpretation as the very lowest. There are at least two possible explanations for this: Firstly, the food producers, of course, have an actual food production, while the specialty food stores in most cases just distribute the food products to the next link (the consumers). The technical specifications of the products are thus naturally more interesting to the foods producers. Even so, this hardly explains why the food producers view 'quality as adaptation to technical specifications' as being more relevant *in the marketplace* than the specialty food stores do. Especially, since their products are directed towards the same customers: the foods consumers. However, another possible explanation is that the food producers are one step behind the specialty food stores in the transformation process. This could be the reason why the foods producers are more inclined to view reality from their own perspective compared to the specialty food stores, which interact more directly with the marketplace.

As mentioned earlier, the companies were also asked to rank the interpretations of quality that they believe their customers (the consumers) regard as most correct (Table 2).

Table 2 shows that the companies do not believe that the consumers are significantly interested in whether the product lives up to the technical specifications. This does not necessarily mean that the consumers are not interested in the uniformity of the products, but could be a result of the companies' tendency to deem the technical specifications too complex for the consumers to understand. Furthermore, it is remarkable that the companies seem to think that the consumers to a large extent perceive quality as excellence. This directly opposes the companies' own perception of quality, which ranks quality as excellence as the least correct interpretation, and it partly opposes the interpretation of the specialty food stores, which ranks quality as fulfillment of expectation above quality as excellence. This could be an indication of 'a quality gap' between the foods companies and their customers: according to the companies, many consumers want excellent food products, but according to themselves the fulfillment of initial expectations (high as well as low) is quite enough.

Table 2. The consumers' supposed interpretation of quality

Interpretations of quality	Study 1 Total#	Rank	Study 2 Total#	Rank
Quality as an excellent product	40	1	336	1
Quality as value	51	3	545	4
Quality as the consumers perceive it	56	4	433	3
Quality as adaptation to expectations	42	2	401	2
Quality as adaptation to technical specifications	81	5	727	5

\# The lowest value indicates the most preferred interpretation of quality

A third question asked the companies to state the importance of quality as a sales variable in relation to other sales variables.

Table 3. The companies' perception of quality as a sales variable

Sales variable	Study 1 Total#	Rank	Study 2 Total#	Rank
Quality is the most important variable	1	3	113	1
Price is the most important variable	8	3	0	4
Price and quality are equally important variable	10	1	40	2
Other sales variables are more important	0	4	10	3

\# The highest value indicates the most preferred option. Only one option per company.

Table 3 shows the interesting point that almost one half of the producers believe that price is the most important sales variable, while none of the specialty food stores share this opinion. Conversely, the specialty food stores see quality as the single most important sales variable, while only one of the producers agree with this opinion. As already mentioned, even though the specialty food stores have traditionally marketed themselves as quality food suppliers, these results represent still remarkable differences between producers and specialty food stores.

6.   CONCLUDING REMARKS

The concept of quality appears fragmented and ambiguous in literature as well as in practice. This is unfortunate. The many main interpretations combined with a great deal of individual interpretations make it difficult for studies that either half-heartedly or completely fail to define the concept of quality to contribute to new theoretical and practical observations. The extraction of general knowledge from results and identification of any contrasts between studies are thus made very difficult. In this way, the results of this study raise the question of why confusion about concepts arises and is maintained, and whether this is a desirable development. Sociolinguists claim that conceptualization corresponds to the reality that you are part of and that ambiguity should be seen as an expression of multiple actors experiencing multiple realities. The view seems sensible, but it only explains why the same word is used for different realities, that is, if a common general concept exists.

We do not wish to argue for a standardization of the concept of quality; the existence of only one interpretation. This would indeed be an unrealistic approach. Thus it is not possible to comment in general about which of the interpretations in Figure 1 is 'better than the others' as this depends on the specific context. The results of the present study, however, highlight the need to define the concept of quality more clearly, so that it becomes consistent with the context wherein it is used. When a company wishes to communicate that they produce and deliver quality products, it is imperative that the company and their customers share the same interpretation of the concept of quality. If this is not the case, the customer will probably not view the communication as intentional. As a common general concept then, quality seems to mean that some people may judge certain things to be better than other things. Since this view will hardly lead to increased recognition, a development of the concept in relation to its reality is called for. Thus there is a need for a linguistic definition, rather than an actual integration of the interpretations into one concept.

REFERENCES

Aaker, David A. (1991), *Managing Brand Equity*, New York: The Free Press.

Abbott, Lawrence (1955), *Quality and Competition*, New York: Columbia University Press.

Abrahamson, Eric (1996), Management Fashion, *Academy of Management*, 21, pp. 254-285.

Assael, Henry (1995), *Consumer Behavior and Marketing Action*, 5th edition, PWS-Kent.

Bagozzi, Richard P. (ed.) (1994), *Principles of Marketing Research*, Blackwell.

Bamberger, Ingolf (1989), Developing Competitive Advantage in Small and Medium-Size Firms, *Long Range Planning*, 22, pp. 80-88.

Bauer, Hans H, Herrmann, Andreas & Gutsche, Jens (1995), Situational variation in brand choice behavior: Results of an empirical study, *Journal of International Marketing & Marketing Research*, 20, pp. 115-127.

Bergman, Bo & Klefsjö, Bengt (1994), *Quality - from Customer Needs to Customer Satisfaction*, London: McGraw-Hill.

Bowbrick, Peter (1992), *The Economics of Quality - Grades & Brands*, Routledge.

Brems, Hans (1951), *Product Equilibrium under Monopolistic Competition, Cambridge*, Mass.: Harvard University Press.

Curry, David J. (1985), Measuring Price and Quality Competition, *Journal of Marketing*, 49, pp. 106-117.

Curry, David J. & Riesz, Peter C. (1988), Prices and Price/Quality Relationships: A Longitudinal Analysis, *Journal of Marketing*, 52, pp. 36-51.

Dale, B.G., Boaden, R.J. & Lascelles, D.M. (1994), Total Quality Management – an overview, In: Dale, B.G., *Managing Quality*, 2. ed., Prentice Hall, New York

Dean, Jr., J.W. & Bowen, D.E. (1994), Management theory and total quality: improving research and practice through theory development, *The Academy of Management Review*, 19, pp. 392-418.

Devlin, Susan J. & H. K. Dong (1994), Service Quality from the customers' perspective, *Marketing Research*, 6, pp. 4-13.

Dodds, William B., Monroe, Kent B. & Grewal, Dhruv (1991), Effects of Price, Brand, and Store Information on Buyers' Product Evaluations, *Journal of Marketing Research*, 28, pp. 307-319.

Dodds, William B. (1995), Market cues affect on consumers' product evaluations, *Journal of Marketing Theory & Practice*, 3, pp. 50-63.

Garvin, David A. (1984), What Does "Product Quality" Really Mean, *Sloan Management Review*, pp. 25-43.

Goetsch, D.L. & Linsay, W.E. (1994), *Introduction to Total Quality*, Merrill.

Grunert, Klaus G., Baadsgaard Allan, Larsen, Hanne Hartvig & Tage Koed Madsen (1996), *Market Orientation in Food and Agriculture*, Kluwer Academic Publishers.

Holbrook, Morris B. & Kim P. Corfman (1985), Quality and Value in the Consumer Experience: Phaedrus Rides Again, in: Jacoby, J & Olson, J. (eds.), *Perceived Quality*, Lexington, MA: Lexington Books.

Jacobson, Robert & Aaker, David A. (1987), The Strategic Role of Product Quality, *Journal of Marketing*, 51, pp. 31-44.

Johnson, Russell D. & Kleiner, Brian H. (1993), Does higher quality mean higher cost?, *International Journal of Quality & Reliability Management*, 10, pp. 64-80.

Jones, Buck (1994), Formula for Succes, *Progressive Grocer*, February, pp. 117-118.

Kirkpatrick, Shelley A. & Locke, Edwin A. (1996), Direct and indirect effects of three core charismatic leadership components on performance and attitudes, *Journal of Applied Psychology*, 81, pp. 36-51.

Kobrin, Stephen J. (1988), Expatriate Reduction and Strategic Control in American Multinational Corporations, *Human Ressource Management*, Spring, 27, pp. 63-75.

Lancaster, Kelvin (1966), A New Approach to Consumer Theory, *Journal of Political Economy*, 84, pp. 132-157.

Lancaster, Kelvin (1971), *Consumer Demand: A New Approach*, New York.

Leavitt H. J. (1954), A note on some experimental findings about the meaning of price, *Journal of Business*, 27, pp. 205-210.

Mintzberg, Henry (1979), *The Structuring of Organizations*, Prentice-Hall, New Jersey.

Neergaard, Peter (ed.) (1998), *New perspectives in quality management*, Samfundslitteratur.

Nilsson, Ole Stenvinkel (1998), Managing Database Marketing Quality, In: Neergaard, Peter (ed.), *New perspectives in quality management*, Samfundslitteratur.

Oakland, J.S. (1993), *Total Quality Management*, Nichols Publishing, New Jersey.

Parzinger, Monica J. & Nath, Ravinder (2000), A study of the relationships between total quality management implementation factors and software quality, *Total Quality Management*, 11, pp. 353-371.

Peterson, Robert A. & Alain J. P. Jolibert (1995), A meta-analysis of country-of-origin effects, *Journal of International Business Studies*, 26, pp. 883-900.

Pirzig, R. M. (1974*), Zen and the art of the motorcycle maintenance*, New York: Bantam Books.

Porter, Michael E. (1980), *Competitive Strategy*, New York, The Free Press.

Reeves, Carol A. & Bednar, David A. (1994), Defining quality: alternatives and implications, *Academy of Management Review*, 19, pp. 419-445.

Rumelt, Richard P. (1974), *Strategy, Structure, and Performance*, Harvard University Press, Cambridge.

Rust, Roland T. & Oliver, Richard L. (1994), *Service Quality: Insights and Managerial Implications From the Frontier. in: Service Quality - New Directions in Theory and Practice*, SAGE Publications.

Rørsted, Bendt (1970), *Anatomies of marketing action within a structure of marketing activity*, doctoral thesis, Universitetsforlaget i Aarhus.

Scott, Richard & Meyer, John W. (1994), *Institutional environments and organizations – structural complexity and individualism*, SAGE Publications.

Snell, Scott A. & Dean, James W., Jr. (1992) Integrated Manufacturing and Human Resource Management: A Human Capital Perspective, *Academy of Management Journal*, 35, pp. 467-504.

Steenkamp, Jan-Benedict E. M., *Product Quality*, Van Corcum, The Netherlands, 1989.

Takeuchi, Hirotaka & John A. Quelch (1983), Quality is more than making a good product, *Harvard Business Review*, July/August, pp. 139- 145.

Tuchman, B. W. (1980), The decline of quality, *New York Times Magazine*, Nov. 2, pp. 38-41.

Zeithaml, Valarie A. (1988), Consumer Perceptions of Price, Quality and Value: A Means-End Model and Synthesis of Evidence, *Journal of Marketing*, 52, pp. 2-22.

Zeithaml, Valarie A., Parasuraman, A og Berry, Leonard L. (1990), *Delivering quality service*, New York: The Free Press.

Chapter 3

STORE IMAGE AND STORE POSITIONS FOR GROCERY RETAIL CHAINS
A correspondence analysis

1. INTRODUCTION

The way a store is perceived by its customers, that is the image of the store, has long been considered as a potentially valuable theoretical construct (Boulding, 1956; and Martineau, 1958). Unlike many issues that are popular predominantly in academic circles store image is believed to have concrete and consequential managerial relevance with regard to its influence on store patronage behavior and hence on store profitability. Trade publications and business media thus characterize store image as a critical determinant of successful retailing (Willmes, 1990; Wilson, 1993).

A consumer's image of a store is not absolute but relative to images of competing stores. Image is a multidimensional construct, because consumers may associate a number of attributes or features, (price level, quality level, service level, etc.) with stores in a competitive market place. Also the overall image of competing stores may vary because of the different attributes that consumers use to differentiate among them. Consumers draw conclusions about a store's overall image from impressions they have of the strengths and weaknesses of the store's service outputs. Images are formed from past experiences, word-of-mouth and marketing communications. As store chains service many different segments of consumers, image assessment becomes important in order to ensure strong patronage. Retailers therefore should be concerned about their store's image and positioning. (For an overview of research on store image refer to Mazursky and Jacoby, 1988; and Lindquist, 1974-1975).

The purpose of this chapter is to investigate the images and positions of eleven grocery retail chains operating in the greater Copenhagen metropolitan area. In particular we want to identify and assess important similarities and differences between the grocery chains and between the different formats of grocery stores operating in this geographical area, and to discuss strategic implications of the results for chain management. The structure of the supermarket market in the Copenhagen metropolitan area corresponds in general terms to the structure of that market in the whole of Denmark. Different formats constitute that market, namely discount stores, hypermarkets and combination stores/conventional supermarkets including up-scale supermarkets. Two large supermarket groups, Dansk Supermarked and COOP Denmark, dominate the Danish supermarket market having a total market share of about 68% in year 2000. The corporate retail chain Dansk Supermarked (market share 25%) is owned by Dansk Supermarked Ltd, whereas COOP Denmark (market share 43%) is a consumer co-op. The Danish independents hold together 28% of the market.

To measure store image we employ correspondence analysis. The basic idea of this methodology in this context is to allow the analyst to compare the grocery chains simultaneously with regard to their store attributes within a multidimensional space.

The chapter is organized into five sections. The next section provides a discussion of issues involved in measuring store image and a presentation of the data. The third section outlines the methodology used in the study. Presentation and discussion of the results follow this in the fourth section. The conclusion and implications are contained in the fifth and final section.

2.   MEASUREMENT OF STORE IMAGE

Many facets of store image have received considerable attention in the retailing literature, including its conceptualization (Kasulis and Lusch, 1981; Keaveney and Hunt, 1992) and operationalization (Golden et al. 1987; Ward et al. 1992; Chowdhury et al. 1998). Whereas some researchers have examined store image as a criterion variable (Baker et al. 1994), others have observed its interactive effects (Thorelli et al. 1989) and its effect as an explanatory variable (Malhotra 1983). The ongoing involvement with store image has generated several debates concerning the theoretical underpinnings of the construct, Chowdhury et al. (1998). Despite these debates a number of complex issues have remained shrouded in ambiguity, however. Some researchers have even described the area as one characterized by a high "noise level", refer to Peterson and Kerin (1983) and Amirani and Gates (1993).

A central area of confusion involves measurement of the construct itself, that is the relationship between the conceptual underpinnings of the image construct and its operationalization. According to Keaveney and Hunt (1992) the application of structured questionnaires using attribute-intensive semantic differentials and the use of attribute based models of information processing combined with the application of multivariate statistical analyses is inappropriate, or at least deficient, for the purpose of measuring store image. Keaveney and Hunt (1992, p. 167) thus argue that "operationalizing retail store image along traditional attribute-based lines cannot account for the 'gestalt'[1] view of store image". Their contention includes the view that individual images of stores are composite, synergistic and gestalt in nature. Therefore, to capture the 'gestalt' of store image they recommend the use of unstructured measurement techniques. However, the use of unstructured measurements of store image is rare, because it is costly and cumbersome. Unstructured questionnaires generally are context sensitive and may yield a different set of measures in different samples, and hence are only of little interest from a managerial point of view. In addition, Chowdhury et al. (1998) demonstrate that the two types of measurements of store image have similar properties, but also that the structured scales are more correlated with self-reported behavioral measures. Against this background we decided to develop "traditional" structured attribute-based scales for the measurement of grocery chain store image.

The development of structured store item scales was conducted systematically in conformance with the standard principles of scale construction, see for instance Churchill (1979) and Gerbing and Anderson (1988). To support our development of scales a review of the current literature on store image provided us with sufficient input to identify a set of scale items to measure the different dimensions of store image, (e.g. Kelly and Stevenson, 1967; Kunkel and Berry, 1968; Lindquist, 1974-1975; Hawkins et al., 1976; Hansen and Deutscher, 1977; Malhotra, 1983; Mazursky and Jacoby, 1986). The final set of twenty-one items used in the questionnaire is shown in Table 1. A seven point scale anchored by (1) = 'strongly disagree' and (7) = "strongly agree" was used for the items.

The images of eleven grocery retail chains operating in the greater Copenhagen metropolitan area were measured using these scales.

---

[1] The term is often used by consumer researchers to convey the idea that an individual's perception of any object incorporates many bits of separate information that are combined in such a manner that the end result of the integration of the inputs amounts to more than the sum of its constituent parts.

Respondents were asked only to evaluate grocery chains they were familiar with. These measurements were part of a much wider investigation of grocery buying behavior in the Copenhagen metropolitan area conducted in the spring of 1999. In all 1500 households were contacted and 631 responded with usable questionnaires resulting in a response rate of 42%. Details of the sampling plan and data collection can be found in Chapter I and in Hansen et al. (1999).

Table 1. Items used for measuring store values

The following store items were measured using a 7-point scale, anchored by (1) Strongly Disagree and (7) Strongly Agree:

a) Broad variety of goods.	k) High service level.
b) Good specials.	l) Good store layout.
c) Good atmosphere.	m) Clean and neat store.
d) Low prices.	n) Always fresh produce.
e) Fast check out.	o) Helpful personnel.
f) Advertise in local papers.	p) Good parking facilities.
g) Long opening hours.	q) Sends out retail circulars.
h) Many new product introductions.	r) Good variety of organic products.
i) High quality level.	s) Good specialty departments.
j) Often taste samples.	t) Easily accessible store.
	u) Good variety of ready-to-eat products.

The eleven grocery chains represent the various store formats that constitute the "supermarket market" in Denmark, namely discount stores, hypermarkets, and conventional supermarkets including combination stores and upscale supermarkets. They make up an important part of the retail grocery market having in total a market share above 70%. Our investigation comprises the following chains: (1) Discount chains, *Netto, Fakta and Aldi.* (2) Hypermarket chains, *BILKA and OBS* (3) Conventional supermarket chains, *Føtex and Kvickly* (combination stores), *ISO* and *Irma* (upscale supermarkets) and SuperBrugsen and Dagli'Brugsen. Nine of these chains are owned by two retailing groups, thus Fakta, SuperBrugsen, Dagli'Brugsen, Irma, Kvickly and OBS are owned by the Danish consumer cooperative COOP Denmark, whereas Netto, Føtex and BILKA are owned by Dansk Supermarked Ltd. ISO and Aldi are independent chains.

3. METHODOLOGY

To analyze consumers' perceptions of grocery chains correspondence analysis was used in combination with cluster analysis. Correspondence analysis is an exploratory multivariate technique that quantifies multivariate data, and produces a graphical representation of the structure in the data. For a discussion of the method in marketing research settings, see Hoffmann and Franke (1986) and Carroll et al. (1986, 1987). The data requirements for correspondence analysis are highly flexible, although the method is ideally suited for categorical data such as "yes-no" or multiple-choice responses. However, the only strict data requirement is in fact a rectangular data matrix with non-negative entries, typically this would be two-way or multiple-way contingency tables.

Mathematically correspondence analysis decomposes the chi-square measure of association between the row and the column categories in the rectangular input matrix in a manner similar to that of principal component analysis for continuous data, (Greenacre, 1984, 1993). The chi-square statistics measures the discrepancy between the *observed* frequencies in a contingency table and the *expected* frequencies calculated under a hypothesis of homogeneity or independence of the relative row frequencies (or the relative column frequencies). The chi-square statistics thus measures how "far" the observed row frequencies are from the expected or average row frequencies. The notion of "farness" is then given a more specific definition in correspondence analysis by defining a distance function, based on this chi-square measure, and it is this matrix of chi-square distances that is the input for a mapping procedure or program similar to a principal component analysis.

The mapping procedure generates n principal components or dimensions and creates the equivalent of a factor score on each dimension for each row variable and each column variable jointly. The name correspondence analysis refers to the fact that row and column scores are reported in corresponding units, which permits the portrayal of the points in joint space and facilitates interpretation. Other multivariate methods lack this ability, (Hoffman and Franke, 1986).

In this study we apply correspondence analysis to the data on consumers' perceptions of grocery chains measured as shown in Table 1. These data are ratings and thus at least ordinal scaled. In order to take the nature of these ratings and the fact that they are bipolar into account, correspondence analysis is applied to a doubled data matrix comprising both the original form and a reflected form of the data. The idea behind doubling is to allocate two complementary sets of data for each rating scale, one labeled the "positive" pole and the other the "negative" pole[2]. Doubling establishes symmetry between the two poles of each bipolar scale such that

---

[2] It is preferred generally to have rating scales with lower endpoint of zero, so the original 1-7 scales were converted to 0-6 scales by subtracting 1 from all the data. Subtracting the converted values from 6 then creates the reflected form of the data.

correspondence analysis becomes invariant with respect to the choice of scale direction -each consumer's response is treated as a positive mass divided between the two poles.

Alternatively we could have re-scaled the data to binary responses and consequently lost much information. Also, we might have applied conventional multiple correspondence analysis which, however, treats the categories of the rating scales as nominal variables and thereby ignores the inherent ordering of the categories.

Lebart (1994) recommends that cluster analysis be conducted to complement the results of correspondence analysis, because of the possibility of shrinkage and/or distortion due to the effect of outliers on the principal dimension in correspondence analysis. The results of cluster analysis are robust against the effect of outliers and can in addition provide more detailed information about the distances between the grocery chains and the store attributes. Therefore, the resulting scores for the attributes and chains were used as input to a cluster analysis to augment the examination of the relationships among the grocery chains and their attributes.

4. RESULTS

The first step in analyzing the results of the correspondence analysis is to determine the number of key dimensions. This involves a trade-off between explanatory power and interpretability. While the interpretability of dimensions is subjective, the explanatory power can be judged by the eigenvalues of the generated dimensions (or factors), which indicate the weighted variance explained (denoted *inertia*) by each of the extracted dimensions.

The dimensionality and its proportion of inertia explained are shown in Table 2. More than 91% of the inertia can be explained by a two-dimensional solution. An additional dimension adds only 4.2% in explained inertia. Therefore this two-dimensional solution is deemed appropriate for further analysis.

The numerical results of the correspondence analysis for the two-dimensional solution are presented in Tables 3a and 3b. This solution is seen also to provide high values of *quality* for all chains and their attributes, that is to say high proportions of category variation explained by the two dimensions.

Because of the large amount of attribute points we consider the attribute map separately before considering a joint map of attributes and chains. Figure 1 shows the attribute points in the two principal dimensions. There are two points for each of the 21 attributes. The positive poles (marked with upper case letters) are directly opposite their negative counterparts (marked

Table 2. The dimensionality and its proportion of inertia explained

Dimension	Inertia	Proportion explained	Cumulative proportion
1	.04082	.796	.796
2	.00613	.119	.915
3	.00216	.042	.957
4	.00112	.022	.979
5	.00040	.008	.987
6	.00025	.005	.992
7	.00021	.004	.996
8	.00015	.003	.999
9	.00005	.001	1.000
10	.00001	.000	1.000
Total	.05130	1.000	1.000

with lower case letters) relative to the origin, as illustrated by the line joining the poles of attribute Aa ("Broad variety of goods – Narrow variety of goods"). The map is constructed such that, if the distance between the poles were to be calibrated in seven equal intervals from 0 at 'a' to 6 at 'A', then the average rating can be read off at the origin (0,0).

Table 3a. Numerical results of correspondence analysis of grocery chains for a two dimensional solution.

Grocery chain	Contribution to inertia		Explanation by dimension		
	Dim. I	Dim. II	Dim. I	Dim. II	Total
SuperBrugsen	0.005	0.035	0.290	0.282	0.572
BILKA	0.015	0.070	0.374	0.270	0.643
IRMA	0.071	0.155	0.608	0.198	0.805
NETTO	0.211	0.229	0.819	0.134	0.953
OBS	0.027	0.087	0.510	0.245	0.755
FAKTA	0.151	0.000	0.988	0.000	0.988
ISO	0.118	0.000	0.949	0.000	0.949
FØTEX	0.074	0.053	0.852	0.091	0.943
Dagli'Brugsen	0.017	0.321	0.214	0.612	0.826
ALDI	0.253	0.042	0.947	0.024	0.971
Kvickly	0.057	0.008	0.946	0.019	0.965
Total	1.000	1.000			

Thus the average rating is seen to be higher than the middle rating point, which indeed appears to be the case for most of the attributes. The relative direction of the lines connecting opposite poles indicate correlation between the attributes, so for instance the fact that D and d ("Low prices – High prices") are oriented opposite to most of the other attributes means that low prices are negatively correlated with them. Also, a relatively long distance between the poles of an attribute indicates that there is more variability in the ratings on that attribute than on attributes where the poles are relatively closer to each other.

Table 3b. Numerical results of correspondence analysis for attributes of grocery chains for a two dimensional solution

Store attribute*	Pole	Contribution to inertia		Explanation by dimen.		
		Dim. I	Dim. II	Dim. I	Dim. II	Total
Variety of goods+	A	0.037	0.018	0.910	0.067	0.977
Variety of goods-	a	0.073	0.036	0.910	0.067	0.977
Specials+	B	0.000	0.070	0.026	0.913	0.939
Specials-	b	0.001	0.129	0.026	0.913	0.939
Atmosphere+	C	0.021	0.000	0.934	0.003	0.937
Atmosphere-	c	0.031	0.001	0.934	0.003	0.937
Low price+	D	0.002	0.095	0.553	0.391	0.944
Low price-	d	0.025	0.117	0.553	0.391	0.944
Check out+	E	0.002	0.049	0.153	0.582	0.735
Check out-	e	0.002	0.045	0.153	0.582	0.735
Advertisements+	F	0.002	0.030	0.263	0.612	0.875
Advertisements-	f	0.003	0.054	0.263	0.612	0.875
Opening hours+	G	0.000	0.033	0.025	0.799	0.824
Opening hours-	g	0.000	0.088	0.025	0.799	0.824
Product introductions+	H	0.004	0.014	0.510	0.242	0.752
Product introductions-	h	0.007	0.022	0.510	0.242	0.752
Quality+	I	0.023	0.001	0.864	0.007	0.871
Quality-	i	0.036	0.002	0.864	0.007	0.871
Taste samples+	J	0.055	0.005	0.838	0.012	0.850
Taste samples-	j	0.048	0.005	0.838	0.012	0.850
Service level+	K	0.040	0.010	0.949	0.034	0.984
Service level-	k	0.045	0.011	0.949	0.034	0.984
Store layout+	L	0.033	0.000	0.959	0.000	0.959
Store layout-	l	0.042	0.000	0.959	0.000	0.959
Clean store+	M	0.026	0.001	0.969	0.007	0.976
Clean store-	m	0.041	0.002	0.969	0.007	0.976
Fresh produce+	N	0.019	0.000	0.915	0.001	0.917
Fresh produce-	n	0.031	0.000	0.915	0.001	0.917
Personnel+	O	0.017	0.004	0.906	0.033	0.939
Personnel-	o	0.022	0.005	0.906	0.033	0.939
Parking+	P	0.005	0.014	0.520	0.208	0.728
Parking-	p	0.010	0.026	0.520	0.208	0.728
Circulars+	Q	0.002	0.029	0.245	0.570	0.815
Circulars-	q	0.004	0.067	0.245	0.570	0.815
Organic products+	R	0.023	0.000	0.900	0.002	0.902
Organic products-	r	0.032	0.000	0.900	0.002	0.902
Specialty departments+	S	0.091	0.002	0.936	0.002	0.938
Specialty departments-	s	0.088	0.001	0.936	0.002	0.938
Accessibility+	T	0.007	0.004	0.874	0.081	0.954
Accessibility-	t	0.013	0.008	0.874	0.081	0.954
Ready-to-eat products+	U	0.009	0.000	0.852	0.000	0.852
Ready-to-eat products-	u	0.010	0.000	0.852	0.000	0.852
Total		1.000	1.000			

*+Refers to positive pole of attribute; upper case letter indicates positive pole
-Refers to negative pole of attribute; lower case letter indicates negative pole

To interpret the dimensions of Figure 1 we need additional information. Figure 1 only shows the projections of the attribute points onto the plane but

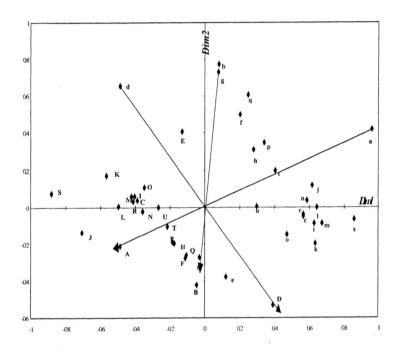

Figure 1. Grocery chain attribute map

does not indicate which attribute have had the most impact in determining the orientation of the dimensions. Table 3b provides the numerical results of the correspondence analysis for the set of attribute points. Each column of the table represents a particular decomposition of the explained variation, i.e. inertia. The relative contributions to inertia quantify the importance of each attribute point in determining the direction of the principal dimension, and serve as guides to the interpretation of each dimension. They are interpreted as the fraction of variance explained by each point in relation to each dimension.

As seen in Table 3b and shown by Figure 1 the first dimension of the attribute space appears to be explained primarily by attributes Aa, Jj, Ss and Cc, Ii, Kk, Ll, Mm, Nn, Rr, which all contribute above the average contribution of 1/21 (4.8%). These attributes represent about 84% of the variation explained by the first dimension, or 67% of the total variation. The positive poles of the attributes may be interpreted as representing *"broad and good product assortment"*, (A=good variety of products; J=often taste samples; R=good variety of organic products, S=good specialty departments), and *"high product and service quality"*, (I=high quality level; N=always fresh produce) and (K=high service quality; C=good atmosphere; L=good store layout; M=clean and neat store).

The second dimension is influenced mainly by attributes Bb, Dd, Ee, Ff, Gg, and Qq, which all contribute above the average. They represent about 81% of the variation explained by the second dimension, or about 10% of the total attribute variation. Considering the positive poles, these attributes may be interpreted as *"low prices/good value"*, (D=low prices) and (B=good specials/discounts; E=fast check-out; G=long opening hours; F=advertise in local newspapers; Q=good circulars).

Because correspondence analysis scales the rows and columns of the input data matrix in corresponding units, the algorithm also can provide a joint map of attributes and grocery chains in the two dimensions as presented in Figure 2. Correspondence analysis thus requires grocery chains that have been rated high on a certain attribute to have a position in the direction of the positive pole of that attribute. Likewise, grocery chains mostly rated high (or low) on the same attributes tend to be close to each other, and attributes characterizing mostly the same grocery chains tend to be close as well. We first note that dimension 1 separates discounts stores (NETTO, ALDI and FAKTA) from the other supermarket formats, while dimension 2 further clearly separates the discount stores. In addition, it appears that the two dimensions moreover separate the group of non-discount stores into the expected groups consisting of, hypermarkets (OBS and BILKA), combination stores (Kvickly and FØTEX), upscale supermarkets (IRMA and ISO) and conventional supermarkets (SuperBrugsen), while Dagli'Brugsen a chain of small conventional supermarkets seems to be positioned away from the other chains.

Also, we note that ISO among all the chains is the one most closely associated with high product and service quality. Though IRMA also appears to have a high product and service quality image, it does not project as distinctive a quality image as does the ISO chain. Furthermore, IRMA seems to be more closely associated with high prices than does ISO.

Figure 2 in addition provides important insights about the group of discount chains, (NETTO, FAKTA and ALDI). Thus NETTO appears most closely associated with low prices, and their image as a low price chain appears to be distinct from the images of the two other discount chains. Clearly FAKTA and ALDI are perceived as being more closely associated with low service, low product- and low store quality than is NETTO. The two hypermarket chains, OBS and BILKA, are perceived rather similarly being associated with good specials, advertising in local newspapers and

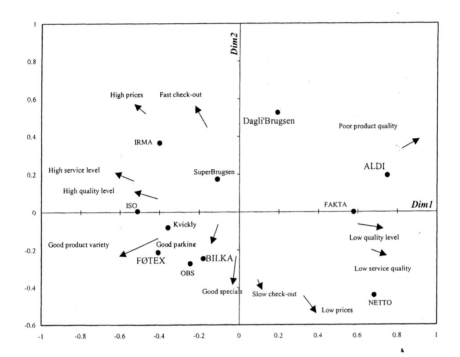

Figure 2. Grocery chain and attribute map

good parking. Also the two combination stores, FØTEX and Kvickly, appear to have an image not very far from the two hypermarkets but more closely related to good product variety and high product and store quality. Finally we note that the two conventional supermarkets, SuperBrugsen and Dagli'Brugsen both appear to occupy not very attractive segments of the map. In particular, Dagli'Brugsen seems not only to be associated with high prices but also situated far away from the positive poles of most attributes.

To shed additional light on the relationship of the grocery chains in terms of their attributes we conducted a hierarchical cluster analysis on the coordinates obtained from the correspondence analysis for chains and attributes. The resulting dendogram is depicted in Figure 3. Generally the dendogram confirms the interpretation of the attribute and chain map, but also provides some additional insight. Thus Irma apparently is being closer to Superbrugsen than to ISO, the alternative high quality or upscale chain.

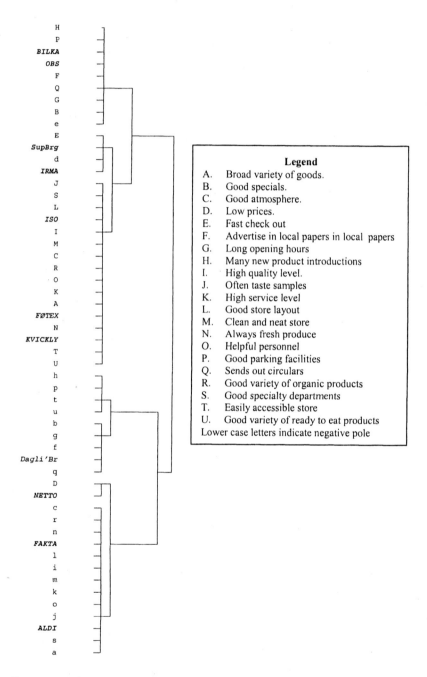

Figure 3. Dendogram of grocery chains and their attributes.

The legend shown in the figure:

Legend

A. Broad variety of goods.
B. Good specials.
C. Good atmosphere.
D. Low prices.
E. Fast check out
F. Advertise in local papers in local papers
G. Long opening hours
H. Many new product introductions
I. High quality level.
J. Often taste samples
K. High service level
L. Good store layout
M. Clean and neat store
N. Always fresh produce
O. Helpful personnel
P. Good parking facilities
Q. Sends out circulars
R. Good variety of organic products
S. Good specialty departments
T. Easily accessible store
U. Good variety of ready to eat products
Lower case letters indicate negative pole

Also, the dendogram confirms that IRMA primarily is perceived as a "high price" chain, and to a lesser degree as a chain with high quality products, service and stores.

The poor image of DagliBrugsen can be further detailed by looking at the dendogram. It is thus interesting to find that Dagli'Brugsen is perceived to be closer to the group of discount stores than it is to the other store formats[3]. Yet, at the same time Dagli'Brugsen is not perceived to be close to the fundamental characteristics of a discount store image, namely low prices and good discounts/specials.

5. CONCLUSION

Although grocery chain image as defined in this paper is a very important aspect of a grocery chain's attractiveness to its customers, there are other equally important factors. Thus the three most important factors in choosing a supermarket were found to be location, location and location, (defined as distance from home or work), followed by price and product variety, that is image variables, (Consumer Reports, 1993). Indeed, the discount chains in Denmark have over the last 15 to 20 years penetrated the market and obtained a considerable share of the market, refer to Table 4, despite the generally poor image they have achieved among consumers as outlined in this paper. This means that the price gaps between the various formats in the 'supermarket market' still are sufficiently large to be major drivers of consumers' decision of where to shop. This observation is supported by a study by Grønholdt et al. (2000), who looked at the relationship between customer satisfaction and loyalty in various industries in Denmark. A key finding in this study is that companies with a low price strategy, as Netto and Fakta, (which are included in their study), appear to have a much higher level of customer loyalty[4] than expected from the level of customer satisfaction they achieve.

The findings of this paper describe how Danish consumers' perceive different grocery chains on twenty-one key store attributes. The perceptual image maps generated by correspondence analysis enables chain management to visualize their chain's competitive advantages and disadvan-

---

[3] The cluster containing Dagli'Brugsen is first clustered with the cluster containing the group of discount stores, before being clustered with other main formats.

[4] Loyalty is measured by four indicators, customer intention to repurchase; intention to purchase another product from the same store chain; intention to switch to a competitor; and intention to recommend the store chain to other consumers.

Table 4. Development of discount grocery chains in Denmark 1991-2002

	1991	1992	2002	2006[*]
Sales in mill DKK				
All grocery chains	63.343	66.523	78.371	NA
Discount chains	9.525	13.228	18.110	NA
Discount in % of all	15,0	20,0	23,1	28,2
No. of stores				
All grocery chains	4.913	3.982	3.388	NA
Discount chains	528	684	829	NA
Discount in % of all	10,7	17,2	24,5	35,9

Source: The Stockmann Group (2001), (2002)
[*]Forecast by Bjerre and Bahr (2002)

tages in relation to their competitors' positions, and to monitor the consequences of their selected strategies to obtain a desired image. It is essential, of course, that there be consistency between a chain's desired image position and the reality inside the store. Thus if a chain wants to be known for its low prices, then it is important for the store to maintain a low-price position in key product categories. Likewise, if a chain has positioned itself as a high-end fresh produce and gourmet store, it is necessary that chain management pay attention to its produce department. Image measurements combined with correspondence analysis as presented in this paper may help management to obtain and maintain a desired image.

REFERENCES

Amirani, S. and Gates, R. (1993), An Attribute-Anchored Conjoint Approach to Measuring Store Image, *International Journal of Retail & Distribution Management,* 21 (5), 30-39.

Baker, J., Grewal D., and Parasuraman, A. (1994), The Influence of Store Environment on Quality Inferences and Store Image, *Journal of the Academy of Marketing Science*, (4), 32 39.

Bjerre, M. and Bahr, H. (2002), Grocery Retail Forecast, Dansk Dagligvare Leverandør Forening, Copenhagen.

Boulding, K.E. (1956), *The Image.* Ann Arbor, MI: University of Michigan Press.

Carroll, J.D., Green, P.E. and Schaffer, C. (1986), Interpoint Distance Comparisons in Correspondence Analysis, *Journal of Marketing Research,* 23, 271-80.

Carroll, J.D., Green, P.E. and Schaffer, C. (1987), Comparing Interpoint Distances in Correspondence Analysis, *Journal of Marketing Research*, 24, 445-50.

Chowdhury, J., Reardon, J. and Srivastava, R. (1998), Alternative Modes of Measuring Store Image: An Empirical Assessment of Structured Versus Unstructured Measures, *Journal of Marketing Theory and Practice,* Spring, 72-86.

Churchill, G.A. (1979), A Paradigm for Developing Better Measures of Marketing Constructs, *Journal of Marketing Research,* 16, 64-73.

Consumer Reports (1993), Survival Guide to the Supermarket, *Consumer Reports*,Vol. 58, No. 9, 559-70.

Gerbing, D.W. and Anderson, J.C. (1988), An Updated Paradigm for Scale Development Incorporating Uni-dimensionality and Its Assessment, *Journal of Marketing Research*, 25, 186-92.

Golden, L., Albaum, G. and Zimmer, M. (1987), The Numerical Comparative Scale: An Economical Format for Retail Image Measurement, *Journal of Retailing*, 63 (4), 393-10.

Greenacre, M.J. (1984), *Theory and Applications of Correspondence Analysis*. NY: Academic Press.

Greenacre, M.J. (1993), *Correspondence Analysis in Practice*. NY: Academic Press.

Grønholdt, L., Martensen, A. and Kristensen, K. (2000), The relationship between customer satisfaction and loyalty: cross-industry differences, *Total Quality Management*, vol. 11, nos. 4/5/6, p. S509-S514.

Hansen, R. and Deutscher,T (1977), An Empirical Investigation of Attribute Importance in Retail Store Selection, *Journal of Retailing*, 52 (4), 59-72.

Hansen, T., Engstrøm, H. and Solgaard, H.S. (1999), Forbrugernes indkøbsadfærd for dagligvarer- en oversigt. WP no. 19, Center for Retailing Studies, Copenhagen Business School.

Hawkins, D.I., Albaum,G. and Best, R. (1976), Reliability of Retail Store Images as Measured by the Stapel Scale, *Journal of Retailing*, 52 (4), 31-38.

Hoffman, D.L. and Franke, G.R. (1986), Correspondence Analysis: Graphical Representation of Categorical Data in Marketing Research, *Journal of Marketing Research*, 23, 213-27.

Kasulis, J.J and Lusch, R.F. (1981), Validating the Retail Store Image Concept, *Journal of the Academy of Marketing Science*, 9 (4), 419-35.

Keaveney, S.M. and Hunt, K.A. (1992), Conceptualization and Operationalization of Retail Store Image: A Case of Rival Middle-Level Theories, *Journal of the Academy of Marketing Science*, 20 (2), 165-75.

Kelly, R.F. and Stevenson, R. (1967), The Semantic Differential: An Information Source for Designing Retail Patronage Appeals, *Journal of Marketing*, 31, 43-47.

Kunkel, J.H. and Berry, L.L. (1968), A Behavioral Conception of Retail Image, *Journal of Marketing*, 32, 21-27.

Lebart, L (1994), Complementary Use of Correspondence Analysis and Cluster Analysis, In *Correspondence Analysis in the Social Sciences*, M.G.A.J. Blasius, ed. NY: Academic Press.

Lindquist, J.D. (1974-75), Meaning of Image: A Survey of Empirical and Hypothetical Evidence, *Journal of Retailing*, 50 (4), 29-38.

Malhotra, N.K. (1983), A Threshold Model of Store Choice, *Journal of Retailing*, 59 (2), 3-21.

Martineau, P. (1958), The Personality of the Retail Store, *Havard Business Review*, 36, 47-55.

Mazursky, D. and Jacoby, J. (1986), Exploring the Development of Store Images,*Journal of Retailing*, 62 (2), 145-65.

Peterson, R.A. and Kerin, R.A. (1983), Store Image Measurement in Patronage Research: Fact and Artifact, in *Patronage Behavior and Retail Management*, W.R. Darden and R.F. Lusch, eds. NY: North-Holland, 293- 306.

Stockmann Group (2001), *Dansk Dagligvarehandel, 10 Årsstatistik 1991-2000.*

Stockmann Group (2002), *Supermarkedshåndbogen 2003.*

Thorelli, H.B., Lim, J.-S. and Ye, J. (1989), Relative Importance of Country of Origin, Warranty and Retail Store Image on Product Evaluations, *International Marketing Review,* 6 (1), 35-46.

Willmes, F. (1990), Continuity Programs Can Boost Store Image, *Supermarket Business,* 45 (3), 89-92.

Wilson, M. (1993), J.C. Penny's New Look, *Chain Store Age Executive,* 69 (6), 70-71.

Chapter 4

A HIERARCHICAL BAYES MODEL OF CHOICE BETWEEN SUPERMARKET FORMATS[*]

1. INTRODUCTION

Understanding the nature of competition among supermarkets is an important area of research in retailing. The supermarket market, in particular, offers the opportunity to study retail competition based on price formats, assortments, and service levels. The grocery retail market is thus in many Western countries dominated by a few supermarket groups each operating a set of store chains primarily differing in pricing policy, assortment and service level, and with a fairly large common set of products and brands.

Grocery supermarket formats are subject to a wide range of variation, (refer to Kahn and McAllister, 1997; Levy and Weitz, 2001), but in this paper we will distinguish between three major formats that we consider span the range of variations in many markets. Conventional supermarkets characterized in general terms by high-low pricing, broad assortment, and some service; discount supermarkets characterized by every-day-low-pricing, narrow assortment and no service, and hypermarkets characterized by a pricing policy somewhat in between the two other formats, wide assortment, and low service. These three formats compete for the major shopping trips of households, and constitute the supermarket market, (Marion, 1998).

[*] Reprinted from Journal of Retailing and Consumer Services, Vol. 10, Solgaard, Hans S. and Torben Hansen, A hierarchical Bayes model of choice between supermarket formats, pp. 169-180, Copyright (2003), with permission from Elsevier Science.

In the positioning of grocery retail stores, price, apparently plays the decisive role, and a much more important role than in the positioning of products and brands. Indeed, 90% of all retail advertising in Europe is price related, and 70% is exclusively on price, (Corstens and Corstens, 1995). This seems to indicate that store choice primarily is motivated by utility considerations rather than by hedonic considerations and that grocery shopping is a functional activity, where consumers' perception of price plays the major role. In a study of consumers' perceptions of grocery retail chains Solgaard (2000), thus observed that although discount chains are rated very poorly compared to other supermarket formats on a whole range of store values except one, namely, good prices, (in all 21 value aspects were rated), discount chains at the same time are growing and gaining market share.

The growing interest in inter format competition in grocery retailing is reflected in a number of recent papers. Lal and Rao (1997) investigate the factors contributing to the success of every-day-low-pricing by analyzing the competition between supermarkets through a game theoretic analysis of a market consisting of time constrained customers and cherry pickers. Bell and Lattin (1998) link consumer preference for shopping in every-day-low-pricing stores versus high-low-price stores to the expected dollar size of the household's shopping basket. Bell et al. (1998) demonstrate how every-day-low-pricing and high-low-pricing stores present shoppers with a trade-off between fixed and variable costs of shopping, and show that high-low-price stores can offer lower total costs for small baskets, while every-day-low-price stores offer lower total costs for large baskets. Finally, Galata, Bucklin and Hanssens (1999) explore the nature of segmentation in store choice behavior where competing supermarkets offer every-day-low-price and high-low promotional price formats. They show contrary to previous research that supermarkets with different price formats may not induce extensive store-format switching among consumers. In this paper we take another look at consumers' choice between different grocery store formats, and investigate the sensitivity of this choice to changes in the consumers' perceptions of the price level, and other variables that influence their decision of which type of store format to patronize. We analyze choice behavior in a Danish setting.

Against this background it is the objective of this paper to model the store choice decision of supermarket shoppers so as to be able to investigate the sensitivity of the store choice decision to changes in shopper's perceptions of the choice determinants. An additional objective is to discuss problems involved in operationalizing store choice models, using the framework of the multinomial logit model, and to suggest alternative model specifications to remedy the identified problems. The multinomial logit model has been widely used in store choice modeling, but also strongly criticized. The primary motivations for rejecting the multinomial logit model in the study of store choice behavior have been the desire to avoid the independence from irrelevant alternatives (IIA) property, and to avoid the assumption that the coefficients of the variables that enter the model take the same values for all consumers.

The remainder of the paper is organized into five sections. The next section provides an outline of the store choice process and of the determinants of choice. Section three discusses problems involved in operationalizing models of store choice using a standard logit framework, and presents a random coefficients logit specification to describe household store choice behavior. The model is operationalized and estimated as a hierarchical Bayes model. The fourth section describes the choice setting and the database utilized to estimate the model. The results of empirical estimations of the model are presented in the fifth section. The results are discussed in the final section six.

2.   STORE CHOICE AND ITS DETERMINANTS

We assume that a consumer's choice of a preferred store format is based on the perceived utility that s/he derives from the store format. In principle the utility emerges based partly on what the consumer perceives s/he receives partly on what the consumers perceives s/he gives. What the consumer receives is in retailing terminology often denoted the store's service output (Bucklin 1966; Bucklin et al. 1996). To receive the service output the consumer will, however, incur some costs, i.e. spend a certain amount of her/his own resources in the form of time and money (Blackwell et al., 2001). Since both resources are scarce we assume that the consumer will try to direct her/his resource consumption toward the store that is perceived to maximize her/his utility, i.e. offering the greatest service output per spend resource unit in the eye of the consumer. This value-for-money perspective (e.g. Chang and Wildt, 1994; Monroe, 1990; Abott, 1955; Hansen, 2001; Sweeney and Soutar, 2001) naturally does not exclude, that some consumers may emphasize service output over 'costs' and select a conventional supermarket or a hypermarket, while others may emphasize 'costs' over service output and prefer to shop in a discount store or hypermarket.

The assessment of the service output is based on the consumer's own experiences with the various store formats. The literature identifies a number of different store values as being potentially significant for the consumer's evaluation of stores, such as merchandise assortment, merchandise quality, service in general, personnel, store lay-out, convenience, cleanliness and atmosphere (Mazursky and Jacoby 1985; Hildebrandt 1988; Blackwell et al. 2001; Levy and Weitz 2001; Bucklin et al. 1996, Finn and Louivere, 1996). The costs that the consumer might incur are determined by the price level and use of time and money resources for transportation to and from the physical store, i.e. a function of the store's location or distance from most often used starting point, (e.g. home or work). A few comments on store values and costs follow.

The overall assessment of a store termed *store image* is a function of the service output offered, of advertising and promotion campaigns as well as of the pricing strategies selected by the store. Since Martineau (1958) store image has constituted a major field of research within retailing, see also Lindquist (1974-75). In the following we consider the importance of the specific store values constituting image rather than the concept per se. For references regarding store image see Peterson and Kerin (1983), Zimmer and Golden (1988), Keaveney and Hunt (1992), Haugtvedt et al. (1992), and Chowdhury et al. (1998).

Store location has received much attention in research on store choice and for good reasons. Bell et al. (1998) refer to industry research in the US that indicates that location explains up to 70 percent of the variations in the choice of grocery store. Refer also to Stanley and Sewall (1976), Verhallen and de Nooij (1982), Engstrøm and Larsen (1987), and Arnold et al. (1983), for the importance of the location or distance variable in store choice. The number and nature of neighboring stores may also be an important factor in the store choice. May (1981) thus argued that consumers tend to make more of their patronage decisions based on the shopping complex instead of the individual store. Hansen and Weinberg's (1979) findings concerning choice of bank outlet support this argument; see also Gripsrud and Horverak (1986). The point is of course that the ease with which the consumer can get from one facility to another type of facility is essential in explaining her choice of store.

Different store formats are derived from combinations of price and service output. Price generally plays the decisive role in the positioning of grocery stores but service outputs, of course, also provide input for the positioning. Retailers can select a price format on a continuum ranging from every-day-low-pricing at one end to high-low-pricing at the other end, but high-low pricing formats generally also provides larger assortments and better service than every-day-low-pricing formats. The choice objects considered in this research are the three retail formats available to consumers in the Danish supermarket market, namely (1) conventional supermarkets characterized by high-low pricing, broad assortment and some service, (2) discount stores characterized by every-day-low-pricing, narrow assortment and no service, and (3) hypermarkets characterized by a pricing format somewhere between (1) and (2), large assortment and some service.

Although an individual consumer alone might perform the chore of grocery shopping, it is the needs of the household that would be satisfied by this activity. Thus household size, and number and age of children will influence store choice behavior. Also, household characteristics such as income, working hours and availability of a car put restrictions on as well as opportunities for what is feasible for the household in terms of grocery purchasing.

2.1   Store utility

The theoretical framework for specifying the process that leads a consumer to choose a certain store from her consideration set of stores is drawn from the theories of consumer behavior developed in marketing (e.g. Blackwell et al., 2001) and from the microeconomic theory of the consumer (e.g. Deaton and Muellbauer, 1980). In line with these theories a consumer is assumed to form *relative* judgments about the available stores based on her/his attitudes towards the stores and on situational considerations. This enables her/him to express her/his behavioral intentions in terms of (perceived) utility assigned to each store. Plans to act are developed according to the assigned utility and a choice is made using a decision rule. We assume that the consumer desires to maximize utility.

Attitude toward a store, in turn is a function of the consumer's perceptions or beliefs (plus the evaluative aspects) of store attributes and her demographic, socioeconomic and personality characteristics. Characteristics of the household, which the consumer belongs to, such as size, and number and age of children are also assumed to influence the attitude formation process. (The household perspective on store choice behavior is specifically developed in Engstrøm and Larsen, 1987). Beliefs in turn are a function of the consumer's evaluative criteria, i.e. store values and information on and experiences with the stores; in addition, beliefs are assumed to be influenced by the general image of the chains operating the stores.

Situational considerations are, finally, a function of the consumer's awareness of events (at the moment of choice) and/or the need to search for information that may affect her choice behavior. Some examples are, (1) upcoming usage situations, that require specific purchases, (see Engstrøm and Larsen, 1987), (2) pressure from competing retailers in terms of various promotional offers that must be evaluated, and (3) shopping activities carried out in combination with other non-domestic activities, creating a possible need for evaluation of   unknown shopping environments, etc. Thus we could also depict the utility assigned to a particular store as a function of store attributes, personal characteristics including relevant household characteristics and situational considerations.

We will assume that the utility assigned to a store is separable into a deterministic attitude component and an unobserved random component. The unobserved random component will include some unmeasured situational influences and random effects in the consumer's information processing, as well as omitted structure. This component thus in essence reflects the complexity and richness of the choice process by recognizing that in building an operational model of the choice decision process the model will in general be under specified.

2.2   From utility to choice.

Most consumers have patterns of grocery shopping which involve more than one store,   (Mägi, 1995; Corstens and Corstens, 1995). Many consumers regularly visit two or more stores simply because they arrange shopping trips from different geographical bases, (e.g. home and work, or other non-domestic activities). Likewise different stores may serve different roles, either by shopping occasion, (e.g. major shopping trip, lunch hour fill-up) or by specialty, (e.g. vegetables, meat, frozen foods, discount, etc.). In addition, some consumers may visit stores on a regular repertoire basis, both to review prices in competing stores and because they enjoy a sense of variety. Still others may visit different stores looking for good values and also in an attempt to track down the items they prefer most. Finally individuals within a household may have different preferences for particular stores.

For these reasons a consumer's consideration set of grocery stores may change from one purchase occasion to another within a short time period such as a week or even a day. A more regular pattern of grocery store choice may, however, emerge over a longer time period such as two weeks or one month. In this paper we consider consumers' buying pattern over the most recent budget period, and measure how consumers share their grocery budget among different store formats, and this pattern we assume to be fairly stable within the shorter run. Since the exact utilities assigned to the different store formats in a consumer's consideration set on a purchase occasion is unknown, we cannot state precisely which store will be selected. However, the probability that the consumer, say i, will select store format j on a particular purchase occasion may be specified as,

$$P_{ij} = \text{prob}\{U_{ij} > U_{ik}; (k \in J, k \neq j)\}$$

where, P_{ij} = probability that consumer i selects store j on a purchase occasion, $U_{ij} = V_{ij} + e_{ij}$ = utility assigned to store j by consumer i, V_{ij} = deterministic component of utility, and e_{ij} = stochastic component of utility, and J = set of stores.

In the following we develop an operationalization of the store choice model summarized above within the framework of the multinomial logit model.

3. OPERATIONALIZATION OF THE STORE CHOICE MODEL.

The multinomial logit model of discrete choice developed by McFadden (1974) has been applied extensively to store choice problems, (e.g. Stanley and Sewall 1976; Gautschi 1981; Malhotra 1983; Arnold et al. 1983, and Fotheringham 1988). There are three important reasons for the widespread use of this model in marketing research, (1) conceptual appeal being grounded in economic theory, (2) analytical tractability and ease of econometric estimation, and (3) excellent empirical performance as measured by model fit and other criteria.

In the logit model, usually specified as standard multinomial logit or nested logit, the stochastic components of the utility function, e_{ij}, are assumed to be identically and independently distributed (IID) in accordance with the extreme value distribution. This specification, however, has some severe limitations. *First* the coefficients of variables that enter the model are assumed to be the same for all consumers. This assumption implies that different consumers with the same *observed* characteristics have the same values or tastes for each factor entering the model. This will generally not be the case. Consumers/households with the same demographic and socioeconomic characteristics, when confronted with a given set of store attributes, may exhibit different choice behavior, because of differences in overall store preferences, and/or variations in their responses to these attributes. Both types of heterogeneity are referred to as "unobserved heterogeneity" because they are the result of the influences of unobserved (to the modeler) factors that influence store choice behavior[1]. *Second* the logit model exhibits the "independence from irrelevant alternatives" (IIA) property, implying that the ratio of the probabilities of choosing one alternative over another is unaffected by the presence or absence of any additional alternatives in the choice set, Domencich and McFadden, (1975).

---

[1] Households with the same observed demographic and socioeconomic characteristics may, as an example, well differ in terms of shared beliefs on how activities concerning food preparation, consumption and purchasing should be carried out, (see for instance Engstrøm and Larsen, 1987).

The primary limitation of models satisfying this property is, that if there are strong contrasts in similarity between the choice alternatives, such models will lead to implausible conclusions when one wants to ascertain the effect of adding a new alternative, or evaluate the effect of changes in an existing alternative. In the context of grocery store patronage the IIA assumption may well be violated[2]. Also, in situations with repeated choices over time the logit and nested logit model assume that unobserved factors or influences are independent over time for a consumer. In reality we will of course expect unobserved factors that affect a consumer to persist at least in the short run.

These limitations are closely related. Thus when the IIA assumption does not hold, the model assumption that has been violated is the assumption that the stochastic element of the utility function is IID, and the reason for this is unobserved heterogeneity. Thus unobserved characteristics (by the modeler) of the consumer may influence how observed characteristics of the consumer and attributes of the alternatives affect choice. Each consumer may as a consequence place their own particular weights on the store attributes (slope heterogeneity), which will lead to correlation across the utility of the store alternatives for each consumer and hence lead consumers to violate the IID as well as the IIA assumption. Moreover, unobserved store attributes will cause correlation in the unobserved portion of utility across store alternatives and hence lead to violation of the IID and the IIA assumptions.

To avoid the IIA assumption we must therefore relax the assumption that the unobserved components of utility are IID. This can be accomplished within the logit model by specifying the unobserved portions of utility as a combination of the IID extreme value term and another distribution, say G, that describes the heterogeneity across consumers. That is each consumer/household has her/its own coefficients for the store attributes and consumer characteristics, and the variation of these parameters across the population is described by the distribution G.

We next outline a random coefficients logit model of store choice. We first describe the behavioral specification, and then briefly consider estimation, use and validation of the model.

---

[2] As an example Fotheringham (1988) mentions that location of a store with respect to its competitors will affect the probability of a consumer selecting that store. If agglomeration forces are present, a consumer is more likely to choose a store in proximity to other stores, cet. par. Alternatively, if competitive forces are present a consumer will be more likely to select a store in relative isolation from its competitors, cet. par.

3.1   A random coefficients logit model of store choice.

Assume a consumer faces a choice set consisting of J stores. The utility that consumer i, say, has assigned to store j is modeled as,

$$U_{ij} = V_{ij} + e_{ij} = \mathbf{X}_{ij}\boldsymbol{\beta}_{ij} + e_{ij} = \Sigma\beta_{il}X_{ilj} + e_{ij}$$

where $\mathbf{X}_{ij}$ is a vector of *observed* store attribute perceptions and household descriptors, whereas $\boldsymbol{\beta}_i$ is a vector of unobserved coefficients for each consumer that varies randomly over the consumers according to a distribution, G. Finally e_{ij} is the unobserved random component independent of $\boldsymbol{\beta}_i$ and $\mathbf{X}_{ij}$. The term e_{ij} is assumed to be distributed IID extreme value. The variance in $\boldsymbol{\beta}_i$ will induce correlation in utility over stores, and the coefficient vector for a consumer, $\boldsymbol{\beta}_i$, may thus be viewed as the sum of a population or market mean $\boldsymbol{\beta}$ representing the average (over all consumers in the market) values or tastes and an individual deviation, $\boldsymbol{\eta}_i$, which represents the consumer's idiosyncratic values. Therefore the unobserved portion of utility is equal to, $\boldsymbol{\eta}_i \mathbf{X}_{ij} + e_{ij}$. This term will be correlated over stores (and purchase occasions) because of the common influence of $\boldsymbol{\eta}_i$, the same values or tastes are used to evaluate each store. (Likewise across purchase occasions at least in the short run). Because the unobserved portion of utility is correlated over stores the random coefficients logit model does not possess the IIA property of the standard logit[3].

Since the exact utilities assigned to the different stores are unknown, we can only specify the *probability* that a consumer, i, will select a particular store on a shopping trip. We can compute the consumer's probability of choosing a particular store, if we know the specific values/tastes of the consumer, $\boldsymbol{\beta}_i$. Since e_{ij} is IID extreme value, as in the standard logit model, McFadden (1974), the probabilities are logit *given* the value of $\boldsymbol{\beta}_i$. Thus the probability that consumer i will choose store j on a choice occasion would be standard logit,

$$P_i(j \mid \boldsymbol{\beta}_i) = \frac{\exp\{\sum_{l=1}^{r}\beta_{il}X_{ilj}\}}{\sum_{k=1}^{J}\exp\{\sum_{h=1}^{r}\beta_{ih}X_{ihk}\}}$$

We next consider how to estimate the unknown parameters $\boldsymbol{\beta}_i$.

---

[3] McFadden and Train (2000) in fact have shown that any random utility model representing any substitution patterns can be approximated arbitrarily close by a random coefficients logit model.

3.2   Estimation of the model.

Advances in computer speed as well as greater understanding of simulation methods, have in recent years allowed estimation of choice model specifications such as the multinomial logit model with coefficients of explanatory variables varying over decisions makers, and in addition estimation of a variety of alternative choice model specifications such as the multinomial probit model and the multinomial t model. Thus Bayesian analysis using Gibbs sampling has recently provided a way to estimate stable individual choice models (Albert and Chib, 1993; Chib et al., 1998; Allenby and Lenk, 1994; Allenby and Rossi, 1999; and McCulloch et al., 2000). Within a Bayesian framework these models estimate the distribution of coefficients across the population and combine information with the individual consumer's choices to derive posterior or conditional estimates of the individual consumer's tastes. Concurrently mixed or random coefficient choice models developed within a classical statistical framework have permitted the same type of analysis by combining maximum likelihood estimates of the population distribution with individual choices, refer to Murthi and Srinivasan (1998), Jain et al. (1994), Chintagunta et al. (1991), Train (1998), and Brownstone and Train (1999). With these advances in estimation procedures it is now possible to estimate choice models that can take care of the problems just outlined.

We have elected to apply Bayesian estimation because it greatly simplifies the interrelated tasks of estimation, inference and communication compared to classical estimation. Thus to learn about a vector of parameters, say β, we simply sample many times from the posterior density for β, and to communicate what we have learned about β from the data we can present summaries of those samples, refer to Jackman (2000) for an introduction to Bayesian simulation.

3.2.1   Bayesian estimation.

We will make the following distributional assumptions in order to be able to estimate the model for an arbitrary consumer. The random effects, $\{\beta_i\}$, for the N consumers are, in the absence of any prior knowledge, assumed to be independently and identically distributed from $N_r(\beta, \Sigma)$, i.e. the r-dimensional multivariate normal distribution with mean vector β and covariance matrix Σ. Using Bayes rule (e.g. Gelman et al. 1995) we obtain information about the household specific parameters β_i, and the common parameters of the mixing distribution β, Σ, by reformulating the likelihood function as a hierarchical Bayes model. The likelihood function is,

$$L(\{\beta_i\}, \overline{\beta}, \Sigma) \equiv \text{prob}(\text{data}|\{\beta_i\}, \overline{\beta}, \Sigma) = \prod_{i=1}^{N} prob\,(\text{data}|\beta_i)\,p(\beta_i|\,\overline{\beta}, \Sigma) =$$

$$\prod_{I=1}^{N} L_i(\beta_i)\,N(\beta_i|\,\overline{\beta}, \Sigma)$$

where i refers to the ith household out of N, $L_i(\beta_i)$ is the likelihood of household i's data conditional on β_i and $p(\beta_i|\,\overline{\beta}, \Sigma) = N(\beta_i|\,\overline{\beta}, \Sigma)$ is the random effects distribution indexed by the parameters, β and Σ. From Bayes rule we know that the "joint posterior distribution of the parameters is proportional to the likelihood times the prior distribution", that is

$$p(\{\beta_i\}, \overline{\beta}, \Sigma|\text{data}) \propto \prod_{I=1}^{N} L_i(\beta_i)\,N(\beta_i|\overline{\beta}, \Sigma)p(\overline{\beta}, \Sigma)$$

In this formulation the mixing distribution is part of the prior distribution, where $p(\beta, \Sigma)$ is a prior distribution placed on β and Σ in order to make sure that the joint posterior distribution will be defined. For convenience we use natural conjugate priors in which the prior on β is normal and the prior on Σ is the inverted Wishart distribution. Convenience refers to the sampling of the posterior distribution, thus assuming β_i to be normally distributed, priors on β and Σ can be specified that give an easy to draw from posterior distribution. Draws from this joint posterior distribution are obtained through Gibbs sampling. That is, a sequence of conditional draws is obtained where each parameter is drawn conditional on a draw from the other parameters, see Casella and George (1992) and Smith and Gelfand (1992) for the Gibbs sampler. In Gibbs sampling draws of β are obtained from its posterior conditional on draws of β_i and Σ for all N. Similarly, draws of Σ are obtained from its posterior conditional on β and β_i for all N. The Gibbs sampling provides a set of draws of β_i from its posterior distribution, and it is the mean of these draws that is the desired parameter 'estimates'. We will not go into further details with the estimation procedure but refer to Allenby and Lenk (1994), Allenby and Rossi (1999), Chib et al. (1998), Huber and Train (2000), and Gelman et al. (1995).

3.3   Measures of choice sensitivity.

Two measures of managerial interest in the context of a logit choice model are the aggregate direct- and cross-choice elasticity measures. Assuming cross-sectional data with only one observation per consumer, as will be the case in our application of the model, the formula for the aggregate choice elasticity for store format j with respect to predictor variable l of store format k is given by

$$E^l_{jk} = \left(\sum_{i=1}^{N} P_{ij} E^l_{ijk} \right) / \sum_{i=1}^{N} P_{ij} ,$$

where, E^l_{ijk} is the choice elasticity for individual i, and

$$E^l_{ijk} = (\delta_{jk} - P_{ik})\beta_{il}x_{ikl},$$

$\delta_{jk} = 1$ if j = k implying a direct elasticity, and
$\delta_{jk} = 0$ if j ≠ k implying a cross elasticity

For derivation of elasticity measures in the logit model refer to McFadden (1979) or Ben-Akiva and Lerman (1985). Estimation in the Bayesian framework is straightforward (Allenby and Lenk 1994; and Jackman 2000). Measures of direct and cross elasticity are estimated for each consumer individually. An aggregate measure of choice sensitivity to, say, a change in perception of a store's price level is then obtained as a weighted average of the posterior distribution of the individual elasticity measures using the choice probabilities as weights.

3.4   Measures of model fit

Model fit will be measured in terms of the fit between the estimated choice probabilities and the observed choices, and in terms of the ability of the model to forecast observed response.

As a measure of the first type, we use the posterior expectation of the deviance, D, (= -2*log(likelihood)), as suggested by Spiegelhalter et al. (1998). To make a connection to classical measures of model fit we compute the log likelihood ratio, λ, based on D and the likelihood at zero, (i.e. $\beta_i = 0$ / $\beta = 0$), except for constants), and compute the 'pseudo' R^2 measure, ρ^2, which can be used much as the R^2 measure in regression, McFadden (1974). To measure fit of the second type we assume that a model specification has been estimated and that a validation sample is available. The proportion of successful individual forecasts made from the validation sample is computed; we forecast that the store with the highest probability will be chosen. To evaluate the performance of the model we compare this proportion to the proportion of successful forecasts we could obtain by chance. We make the predictions given observations of X_{ij} from the validation sample by sampling from the posterior distribution of β_i, (β for the standard logit model), estimated in the calibration sample. The predictions of the percent correct classified is then the average percent correct classified across the number of iterations performed.

4.   CHOICE SETTING AND DATA

To illustrate estimation of the store choice model, data were generated from a survey of grocery buying behavior conducted in the greater Copenhagen metropolitan area in the spring of 1999. The target population consisted of households. In all 1500 households were contacted and 631 responded with useable questionnaires resulting in a response rate of 42%. Information on the sampling plan, data collection and variable construction is provided in   Hansen et al. (1999). In the following we briefly describe the choice setting, and delineate the variables provided by the survey and utilized in building the criterion and predictor variables.

4.1   The choice setting

Marion (1984,1998) has suggested that the grocery retail market may be partitioned into eight strategic groups which each offer a unique combination of price, service and assortment. Three of these groups are in competition for consumers' major grocery shopping; these three groups constitute the "supermarket market". The remaining three groups compete in "the fill in market". The supermarket market in the greater Copenhagen metropolitan area can be described by the general structure of that market in Denmark. Different formats constitute this market, namely discount stores, hypermarkets and combination stores/conventional supermarkets including up-scale supermarkets. Two large supermarket groups, Dansk Supermarked and COOP Denmark, dominate the Danish supermarket market having a total market share of 68% (2000). The corporate retail chain Dansk Supermarked (market share 25%) is owned by Dansk Supermarked Ltd, whereas COOP Denmark (market share 43%) is a consumer co-op. The Danish independents hold together 28% of the market. Of the independents 55% are joined in wholesale-sponsored voluntary cooperative groups, whereas 32% are joined in retail-sponsored cooperatives. Aldi the German discount store chain holds a market share of 4% of the supermarket market.

Dansk Supermarked comprises the discount store chain Netto (market share 10%), the hyper-market chain BILKA (market share 5%), and the combination store/conventional super-market chain FØTEX (market share 10%). COOP Denmark operates the discount store chain Fakta (market share

10%), the hypermarket chain OBS (market share 3%), the combination store/conventional supermarket chain Kvickly (market share 9%), the conventional supermarket chains SuperBrugsen (market share 16%) and Dagli'Brugsen (market share 5%), and the up-scale conventional supermarket chain IRMA (market share 2%). The Danish independents, among them the up-scale chain ISO, comprise conventional supermarkets (total market share 22%), discount supermarkets (total market share 4%) and others (market share 2%).

In the following we model households' choice between different store formats, namely (a) discount stores represented by (NETTO, Fakta and Aldi), (b) hypermarkets represented by (BILKA and OBS), and (c) conventional supermarkets represented by (ISO, IRMA, Kvickly, FØTEX and SuperBrugsen).

4.2   The data

The *predictor variables* provided by the survey consist of measures of consumers' perceptions of store values, a distance measure and household descriptors. The store perceived variables were developed from consumers' ratings of each of the ten grocery store chains listed above using structured attribute-based scales, see Solgaard (2000) for details. In all twenty-one store values or items were used in the questionnaire, each item being evaluated on a seven-point scale anchored by (1) "Strongly disagree" and (7) "Strongly agree", see Table 1. Principal component analysis (PCA) was performed on each of the sets of value measurements and indicated that the structures of the store images was fairly similar across the ten stores. Five components were extracted.

Table 3. Items used for measuring store values

The following store items were measured using a 7-point scale, anchored by (1) Strongly Disagree and (7) Strongly Agree:

a)	Broad variety of goods.	k)	High service level.
b)	Good specials.	l)	Good store layout.
c)	Good atmosphere.	m)	Clean and neat store.
d)	Low prices.	n)	Always fresh produce.
e)	Fast check out.	o)	Helpful personnel.
f)	Advertise in local papers.	p)	Good parking facilities.
g)	Long opening hours.	q)	Sends out retail circulars.
h)	Many new product introductions.	r)	Good variety of organic products.
i)	High quality level.	s)	Good specialty departments.
j)	Often taste samples.	t)	Easily accessible store.
		u)	Good variety of ready-to-eat products.

Summated scales were developed, such that each component is represented by surrogate variables selected among the highest loading original variables on each component. A simple average of the substitute variables represents each component in the choice model, for development of summated scales refer for instance to Hair et al. (1998).

The following store perception variables were included in the model; *price* level (variables b, d, see Table 1) before inclusion in the model this variable was rescaled such that high ratings imply high price level; *quality/service* level (variables i, k, n, see Table 1) scaled such that high ratings imply high quality/service level; *opportunity to taste/try new products* (variables j, u, see Table 1), scaled such that high ratings imply good opportunities to try; *assortment* (variables a, h, see Table 1), scaled such that high ratings imply good assortment; *accessibility* (variables p, t, see Table 1) scaled such that high ratings imply good accessibility.

Distance to store was measured in minutes of transportation time, as estimated by the consumer from most often used starting point, either home or job. A store format's perceived service output is thus represented in the model by the variables quality/service-level, assortment, opportunity to try new products and accessibility, whereas the perceived costs are price-level and distance.

Household/consumer descriptors were also available, and to test the effect of various such variables on the store choice decision, we considered three household descriptors. They are household size, i.e. number of persons in the household, age of person who most often performs the grocery shopping, and household gross income.

The *criterion* variable was developed from data on each household's stated patronage of the ten grocery store chains and from data on the household's stated share of purchases in terms of spending in the different store chains; each household was asked to indicate for each of the ten store chains the approximate percentage of their grocery budget that was spent in the particular store. The store with the highest share of purchases among the stores visited by a household was defined as the chosen store, while the choice set for a household was defined as the set of stores with a positive share of purchase[4].

---

[4] Alternatively we could have used the stated budget shares as the criterion variable. However, we chose to define the criterion variable as delineated above to partly account for errors made in reporting the budget shares. Thus while the stated share of budget for the primary store may be reliable, the stated budget shares for the secondary stores generally may be less reliable, in particular, the stated differences in budget share between these stores may be unreliable.

The sample included 631 households. 524 households indicated a choice set comprising the three store formats under consideration. Of these 112 were eliminated due to incomplete information, leaving a total of 412 respondents. A validation sample consisting of twenty percent of this sample, i.e. 82 households, was formed by random selection, leaving a calibration sample of 330 households. The choice shares for the three store formats are shown in Table 2.

Table 1. Choice shares for the three store formats

a. *Calibration sample n=330*		b. *Validation sample n=82*	
Discount stores (alternative 1)	0.45	Discount stores (alternative 1)	0.45
Hypermarkets (alternative 2)	0.12	Hypermarkets (alternative 2)	0.11
Conventional supermarkets (alternative 3)	0.43	Conventional supermarkets (alternative 3)	0.44

5.   MODEL ESTIMATION AND RESULTS

We next present the results of the empirical estimations of the store choice model. We consider two specifications of the logit model that is the standard- or fixed coefficients logit model and a mixed – or random coefficients logit model. Both models are estimated applying Bayesian simulation, specifically we use the WINBUGS program (Spiegelhalter et al., 2000; Lunn et al., 2000) to perform the simulations and estimations.

We have set the alternative, conventional supermarkets, as the base alternative, and thus include two alternative specific constants in the estimations. The constant for discount stores, (C-DS in Tables 3 and 4), thus reflects the difference in utility of discount stores compared to conventional supermarkets ceteris paribus, similarly for the alternative specific constant for hypermarkets, (C-HM in Tables 3 and 4). Also the difference between the two constants reflects the difference in utility between discount stores and hypermarkets.

Table 3 presents a standard logit model with six generic variables. We note that the parameter estimates and the auxiliary measures of goodness of fit obtained for the standard logit model using Bayesian simulation are very similar to the estimates obtained using maximum likelihood estimation. In fact the estimates only deviated on the third or fourth decimal. We ran the Gibbs sampler for 5.000 iterations to adapt the program. The posterior means, i.e. the parameter estimates and goodness of fit measures are based on the next 30.000 iterations. The fit of the model specification as measured by the likelihood ratio statistic is significant beyond the 0.01 level. In addition the average out of sample percent correct predicted choices are significantly better than the percent correct predicted using a chance criterion. Also the significant coefficients of the generic variables, price,

assortment, accessibility and distance all have the expected sign. The
negative constant terms indicate that conventional supermarkets are the
preferred store format. We found furthermore that the three house- hold
descriptors described above did not have a significant effect on the choice
probabilities. These variables were entered into the model as alternative
specific variables.

Table 2. Standard logit model parameter estimates (posterior standard deviation)

Variable	Coefficient (β)	t
Quality/Service level	-0.1762	-1.51
	(0.117)	
Price level	-0.4874	-4.69
	(0.104)	
Samples	0.1114	1.08
	(0.103)	
Assortment	0.8192	5.46
	(0.150)	
Accessibility	0.1677	1.68
	(0.100)	
Distance	-0.2791	-4.13
	(0.067)	
C-DS	-0.6337	-2.36
	(0.269)	
C-HM	-0.8505	-3.55
	(0.239)	
Summary statistics:		
Number of observations:	330	
Bayesian Deviance, D:	460.5 (4.03)	
-2*loglikelihood at zero D_0:	645.7	
$\rho^2 = 1 - (D/ D_0)$:	0.2868	
Percent correct classified from validation sample:	64% (0.024)	
Percent correct classified using chance criterion:	45%	

A priori it is doubtful that all households would place the same value on
each of the store attributes. To account for this we estimate a random
coefficients logit model for the choice between store formats. We assume the
coefficients are normally distributed that is, $\beta_i \sim N(\overline{\beta}, \Sigma)$. As discussed in
section 3 priors for the parameters β, Σ are introduced to insure that the
posterior distribution is defined. As strongly suggested by the WINBUGS
manual we use conjugate priors, so the prior on β is taken to be normal, and
the prior on Σ is the inverted Wishart. We attempted to use "flat" or diffuse
priors for β and Σ because of lack of information on these parameters. More
precisely we specify the priors with the following parameters, mean(β)
=1.0, and the inverse Wishart as IW(R(8,8), k=12). We found, however, our

results to be sensitive to changes in k, the degrees of freedom in the Wishart distribution. Specifically, we found our results to be *insensitive* to values of k in the interval (9-15), meaning that we did obtain parameter estimates that did not differ significantly on the first two digits. For k>15 this did not hold. We chose to set k=12 to have some degrees of freedom. We ran the Gibbs sampler for 15.000 iterations to adapt the program. The posterior means are based on the next 70.000 iterations. Since autocorrelation appeared to be a problem in the sampling process, we started the process from three different sets of starting values, but found all three chains to give very similar posterior means.

Parameter estimates as well as measures of goodness of fit for the hierarchical Bayes model are reported in Table 4. The mean of the normal random effects distribution is reported as well as the variance estimates of the random effects. The covariance terms of the random effects are all insignificant and small, and therefore not reported. We note that we also in this specification found the three household descriptors to be insignificant.

We first notice that the parameter estimates for the variables *price, distance and assortment* are significant at the 5% level or beyond, and that *accessibility* appears to be significant at the 10% level. Further we note that the coefficients of the random parameters model generally appear to be larger in magnitude than the corresponding standard logit estimates. This is because the scale of the coefficients in logit models is determined by the normalization of the unobserved portion of utility, i.e. e_{ij}. In the random parameters logit some of the utility that is unobserved in the standard logit (and thus captured by e_{ij}) is captured by the standard deviation terms. Thus random parameters logit is scaled to an unobserved portion of utility that has less variance than that for the standard logit, and resulting in the random parameters logit coefficients to be scaled up relative to the standard logit.

Secondly, we observe that the variance estimates reveal several significant (at the 10% level or beyond) or close to being significant elements, indicating the extent of heterogeneity among households in sensitivities to price-level and distance in particular, and in assortment and accessibility, a heterogeneity which the standard logit model is unable to capture. Generally the random coefficients model appears to be a clear improvement over the standard logit specification. This is supported by the clear improvement in model fit as measured by the Bayesian deviance, by the likelihood ratio index ρ^2 and by the improvement in the average out of sample percent correct classified, changing from 64% in the fixed effects model to 71% in the random effects model. These results indicate a clear need for individual specific parameter estimates.

Table 3. Hierarchical Bayes model parameter estimates (posterior standard deviation)

Variable	Coefficient (β)	t	Variance (Σ)	t
Quality/Service	-0.2255	-1.21	0.3741	1.26
level	(0.187)		(0.297)	
	-0.6935	-4.23	0.2196	1.64
Price level	(0.164)		(0.134)	
	0.1703	1.10	0.2318	1.49
Samples	(0.155)		(0.155)	
	1.2370	4.98	0.2266	1.43
Assortment	(0.248)		(0.158)	
	0.2919	1.76	0.2429	1.47
Accessibility	(0.166)		(0.165)	
	-0.4637	-3.86	0.2101	1.95
Distance	(0.120)		(0.108)	
	-0.8098	-2.27	0.3664	0.80
C-DS	(0.356)		(0.456)	
	-0.9790	-3.32	0.3387	1.07
C-HM	(0.295)		(0.315)	

Summary statistics:

Number of observations:	330
Bayesian deviance, D:	329.7 (31.2)
-2*Loglikelihood at zero, D_0:	645.7
$\rho^2 = 1 - (D/D_0)$:	0.4894
Percent correct classified from validation sample:	71% (0.045)
Percent correct classified using chance criterion:	45%

6. DISCUSSION AND CONCLUSION

Price level, assortment and distance (location) appear as anticipated to be the important drivers for consumers' choice between store formats. Quality and service on the other hand do not differentiate between formats. A main reason for this last result could be that the majority of stores that constitutes the choice set belongs to one of only two supermarket groups, and that there is a fairly large common set of standardized products and brands between store chains across store formats. Further it is noted that the importance of 'distance' varies the most across consumers. This should be seen in the light that discount stores and conventional supermarkets in many areas of the metropolitan region under consideration are situated in close proximity to each other. Thus for many small households and households without a car the perceived marginal costs of shopping at a hypermarket located far away may well exceed the perceived benefits. Finally, assortment appears to be the most important single driver for the choice between store formats. A reason

Table 4. Aggregate, direct- and cross- choice elasticities for hierarchical Bayes model (posterior standard deviation)

Store format	DS	HM	CS
		Price Sensitivity	
Discount store (DS)	-0.95	0.74	0.65
	(0.23)	(0.19)	(0.14)
Hypermarket (HM)	0.18	-1.23	0.16
	(0.05)	(0.32)	(0.05)
Conventional Supermarket (CS)	0.58	0.56	-0.76
	(0.14)	(0.18)	(0.19)
		Assortment Sensitivity	
Discount store (DS)	1.48	-1.15	-1.21
	(0.27)	(0.23)	(0.23)
Hypermarket (HM)	-034	2.54	-0.37
	(0.07)	(0.48)	(0.08)
Conventional Supermarket (CS)	-1.29	-1.29	1.70
	(0.24)	(0.25)	(0.31)
		Distance Sensitivity	
Discount store (DS)	-0.36	0.30	0.29
	(0.09)	(0.10)	(0.07)
Hypermarket (HM)	0.10	-0.77	0.11
	(0.03)	(0.23)	(0.04)
Conventional Supermarket (CS)	0.30	0.38	-0.42
	(0.07)	(0.12)	(0.10)

for this could be that we consider the most preferred and chosen store (and thus the selected store format) as the store in which the consumer spends the largest share of the household's grocery budget. That is to say that the chosen store generally also will be the target for the household's major shopping trip in the considered period, and thus a wide and good assortment means that the grocery shopping can be done in a single store.

Table 5 presents the mean direct and cross elasticity of choice probabilities with respect to perceived price, perceived assortment and distance with the posterior standard deviations in parenthesis. The table provides additional insight into the competition between the store formats. The hypermarket format generally has the largest direct elasticity (entries in the diagonal) for the three variables, followed by the discount format and conventional supermarket format. On the other hand an analysis of the off diagonal entries, the cross elasticities, reveal which store format is most influenced by changes in a competitor's store values. For price the discount format appears to have the greatest influence, while the conventional supermarket format exerts the largest effect with respect to assortment.

Concerning distance the hypermarket format seems to be the most sensitive and the least influential.

For store or chain management the store choice model allows for an assessment of a store's competitive situation at a given point in time or across a well defined time period, depending on the data input. A store's strengths and weaknesses on important store attributes and in addition on various aspects of these store attributes may thus be evaluated. The diagnosis of the competitive situation may then serve as the basis for formulation of marketing strategies. To derive specific managerial implications in terms of actions that for instance store management could engage in to improve its store's competitive situation, we would need estimates of the costs and benefits involved in changing the consumers' perception of various aspects of store attributes from their current levels. For instance the substantive problem of measuring the effect of a change in an aspect of store assortment for a particular store-outlet on consumers' perceptions of the store, and hence choice of store, can be tackled by our store model in combination with conjoint analysis.

Conjoint analysis can provide a translation of changes in objective store attributes into changes in perceptions. Via the store model the effect of the specific design change on store choice behavior can then be assessed.

In this paper we have shown how some of the major problems in operationalizing store choice models using the framework of the logit model potentially could be overcome by an alternative model specification, the random parameters or coefficients logit model, and we have demonstrated how hierarchical Bayes estimation appear to be an effective way of estimating random utility models. We presented an application of the store choice model, analyzing households' choice between different formats of grocery retail stores. The application demonstrated the potential usefulness of the random coefficients logit model as compared to the standard logit model.

REFERENCES

Abbott, L. (1955), *Quality and Competition,* Columbia University Press, NY.
Albert, J.H. and S. Chib (1993), "Bayesian Analysis of Binary and Polychotomous Response Data", *Journal of the American Statistical Association,* vol. 88,no. 422, 669-79.
Allenby, G.M. and P.J. Lenk (1994), "Modeling Household Purchase Behavior With Logistic Normal Regression", *Journal of the American Statistical Association,* vol. 89, no. 428, pp. 1218-1231.
Allenby, G. M. and P.E. Rossi (1999), "Marketing models of consumer heterogeneity", *Journal of Econometrics,* 89, pp. 57-78.
Arnold, S.J., T.H. Oum and D.J. Tigert (1983), "Determinant Attributes in Retail Patronage:

Seasonal, Temporal, Regional, and International Comparisons," *Journal of Marketing Research*, 20, 149-157.

Bell, D.R. and J.M. Lattin (1998), "Shopping Behavior and Consumer Preference for Store Price Format: Why "Large Basket" Shoppers Prefer EDPL, *Marketing Science*, 17, 66-88.

Bell, D.R., T.-H. Ho and C.S. Tang (1998), "Determining Where to Shop: Fixed and Variable Costs of Shopping", *Journal of Marketing Research* 35, 352-369.

Ben-Akiva, M. and S.R. Lerman (1985), *Discrete Choice Analysis*, the MIT Press, Cambridge, MA.

Blackwell, R.D., P.W. Miniard and J.F. Engel (2001), *Consumer Behavior*, Ninth ed., Harcourt, Forth Worth.

Brownstone, D. and K. Train (1999), "Forecasting New Product Penetration with Flexible Substitution Patterns," *Journal of Econometrics*, 89, 109-129.

Bucklin, L.P. (1966), *A Theory of Distribution Channel Structure*, Institute of Business and Economic Research, Berkeley, CA.

Bucklin, L.P., V. Ramaswamy and S.K. Majumdar (1996), "Analyzing Channel Structures of Business Markets Via the Structure-Output Paradigm", *International Journal of Research in Marketing*, 13, 73-87.

Casella, G. and E.I. George (1992), "Explaining the Gibbs Sampler", *The American Statistician*, vol. 46, no. 3, pp. 167-174.

Chang, T-Z and A.R. Wildt (1994), "Price, Product Information, and Purchase Intention: An Empirical Study", *Journal of the Academy of Marketing Science*, 22, 16-27.

Chib, S., E. Greenberg and Yuxin Chen (1998), "MCMC Methods for Fitting and Comparing Multinomial response Models", Working paper, Washington University, St. Louis, MO.

Chintagunta, P.K, D.C. Jain and N.J. Vilcassim (1991), "Investigating Heterogeneity in Brand Preferences in Logit Models for Panel Data." *Journal of Marketing Research*, 28, 417-428.

Chowdhury, J., J. Reardon and R. Srivastava (1998), "Alternative Modes of Measuring Store Image: An Empirical Assessment of Structured Versus Unstructured Measures," *Journal of Marketing Theory and Practice*, vol. 6, no. 2, 72-86.

Corstens, J. and M. Corstens (1995), *Store Wars, The Battle for Mindspace and Shelfspace*. Chichester: Wiley & Sons.

Deaton, A. and J. Muellbauer (1980), *Economics and consumer behavior*, Cambridge University Press, London.

Domencich, T.A. and D. McFadden (1975), *Urban Travel Demand, A Behavioral Analysis*, Amsterdam: North-Holland Publishing Co.

Engstrøm, H. and H.H. Larsen (1987) *Husholdningernes Butiksvalg: Indkøbsadfærd for Dagligvarer*. København. Nyt Nordisk Forlag.

Finn, A. and J.J. Louviere (1996), "Shopping Center Image, Consideration, and Choice: Anchor Store Contribution", *Journal of Business Research*, 35, 241-251.

Fotheringham, A.S. (1988), "Consumer Store and Choice Set Definition," *Marketing Science*, vol.7, no.3, 299-310.

Galata, G., R.E. Bucklin and D.M. Hanssens (1999), "On the Stability of Store Format Choice". Working paper, Anderson School at UCLA.

Gautschi, D.A. (1981), "Specification of patronage Models for Retail Center Choice." *Journal of Marketing Research* 18, 162-174.

Gelman, A., J.B. Carlin, H.S. Stern and D.B. Rubin (1995), *Bayesian Data Analysis*, Chapman & Hall/CRC, Boca Raton.

Gripsrud, G. and Ø. Horverak (1986), "Determinants of retail patronage: A 'natural' experiment", *International Journal of Research in Marketing*, 3, 263-272.

Hair, J.F, R.E. Anderson, R.L. Tatham and W.C. Black (1998), *Multivariate Data Analysis*,

Fifth ed, Prentice-Hall, International, NJ.

Hansen, T. (2001), "Quality in the Market Place: A Theoretical and Empirical Investigation," *European Management Journal,* 19, 203-211.

Hansen, T., H. Engstrøm and H.S. Solgaard (1999), "Forbrugernes indkøbsadfærd for dagligvarer- en oversigt." CDS Working Paper, Copenhagen Business School.

Hansen, M.H. and C.B. Weinberg, (1979) "Retail market share in a competitive market," *Journal of Retailing,* 55, 37-46.

Haugtvedt, C., R.E. Petty and J.T. Cacioppo (1992), "Need for Cognition and Advertising: Understanding the Role of Personality Variables in Consumer Behavior," *Journal of Consumer Psychology,* 1, 239-260.

Hildebrandt, L. (1988), "Store Image and the Prediction of Performance in Retailing", *Journal of Business Research,* 17, 91-100.

Huber, J. and K. Train (2000), "On the Similarity of Classical and Bayesian Estimates of Individual Mean Parthworths", Working paper, Department of Economics, UC, Berkeley.

Jackman, S. (2000), "Estimation and Inference Are Missing Data Problems: Unifying Social Science via Bayesian Simulation," *Political Analysis,* 8:4, 307-32.

Jain, D.C., N.J. Vilcassim and P.K. Chintagunta (1994), "A Random Coefficients Logit Brand Choice Model Applied to Panel Data." *Journal of Business & Economic Statistics,* 12,3, 317-328.

Kahn, B.E., and L. McAlister (1997), *Grocery Revolution: The New Focus on the Consumer.* N.Y.: Addison-Wesley.

Keaveney, S.M. and K.A. Hunt (1992), "Conceptualization and Operationalization of Retail Store Image: A Case of Rival Middle-Level Theories," *Journal of the Academy of Science,* 20 (2), 165-175.

Lal, R. and R. Rao (1997), "Supermarket Competition: The Case of Every Day Low Pricing," *Marketing Science,* 16, 60-80.

Levy, M. and B. Weitz (2001), *Retailing Management,* 4th edition, McGraw-Hill/Irwin

Lindquist, J.D. (1974-75), "Meaning of Image: A Survey of Empirical and Hypothetical Evidence," *Journal of Retailing,* 50(4), 29-37.

Lunn, D.J., A. Thomas, N. Best and David Spiegelhalter (2000), "WinBUGS – A Bayesian Modelling framework: Concepts, structure, and extensibility" *Statistics and Computing,* 10, pp. 325-37.

Malhotra, N.K. (1983), "A Threshold Model of Store Choice," *Journal of Retailing,* 59, 2 3-21.

Marion, B.W. (1984), Strategic Groups, Entry barriers and Competitive Behavior in Grocery Stores, *Journal of Retailing,* vol. 59, no.3, pp. 49-75.

Marion, B.W. (1998), Competition in Grocery Retailing: The Impact of a New Strategic Group on BLS Price Increases. *Review of Industrial Organization,* 13, pp.381-99.

Martineau, P. (1958), "The Personality of the Retail Store," *Harvard Business Rview,* 36 (january-february).

May, E.G. (1981), "Product positioning and segmentation strategy: Adaptable to retail stores? In: R.W. Stampfl and E.C. Hirschman (eds.), Theory in retailing: traditional and nontraditional sources: Chicago: AMA, 144-153.

Mazursky, D. and J. Jacoby (1985), "Exploring the Development of Store Images", *Journal of Retailing,* 62, 145-165.

McCulloch, R.E., N.G. Polson and P.E. Rossi (2000), "A Bayesian analysis of the multinomial probit model with fully identified parameters",*Journal of Econometrics,* 99, 173-93.

McFadden, D. (1974), "Conditional logit analysis of qualitative choice behavior." In: P. Zarembka (ed.) *Frontiers in Econometrics,* N.Y.: Academic Press.

McFadden, D. (1979), Quantitative methods for analyzing travel behavior of individuals: Some recent developments. In: Hensher and Stopher (eds.), *Behavioral travel modeling.* London: Croom Helm.

McFadden, D. and K. Train (2000), "Mixed MNL Models for Discrete Response." *Journal of Applied Econometrics, vol. 15, no. 5, 447-470.*

Monroe, K.B. (1990), *Pricing: Making Better Profitable Decisions,* McGraw-Hill, NY.

Mägi, A. (1995), *Customer satisfaction in a store performance framework.* EFI Research Report, Stockholm: Economic Research Institute.

Murthi, B.P.S. and K. Srinivasan (1998), "Performance of the integrated random coefficients covariance probit model: Implications for brand choice." *International Journal of Research in Marketing,* 15, 137-156.

Peterson, R.A. and R.A. Kerin (1983), "Store Image Measurement in Patronage Research: Fact and Artifact," in Darden, W.R., and R.F. Lusch (eds.), *Patronage Behavior and Retail Management,* N.Y.: Elsevier.

Smith, A.F.M. and A.E. Gelfand (1992), "Bayesian Statistics Without Tears: A Sampling – Re-sampling Perspective", *The American Statistician,* Vol. 46, no. 2, pp. 84-88.

Solgaard, H.S. (2000), "Consumers' Perceptions of Grocery Retail Chains: A Correspondence Analysis Approach" in E. O. Martinez, L. G. Ruiz and E.P. del Campo (eds.), *Proceedings from the III International Forum on the Sciences, Techniques and Art Applied to Marketing,* Madrid, pp 161-71.

Spiegelhalter, D., N.G. Best and B.P. Carlin (1998), "Bayesian deviance, the effective number of parameters, and the comparison of arbitrarily complex models", http://www.mcd.ic.ac.uk

Spiegelhalter, D., A. Thomas, and N.G. Best (2000), *WinBUGS User Manual* http://www.mrc-bsu.cam.ac.uk/bugs.

Stanley, T.J. and M.A. Sewall (1976), "Image Inputs to a Probabilistic Model. Predicting Potential," *Journal of Marketing* 40, 48-53.

Sweeney, J.C. and G.N. Soutar (2001), Consumer Perceived Value: The Development of a Multiple Item Scale, *Journal of Retailing,* 77, 203-220.

Train, K. (1998) "Recreation Demand Models with Taste Differences over People," *Land Economics,* 74,2, 230-239.

Verhallen, T.M.M. and G.J. de Nooij (1982), "Retail Attribute Sensitivity and ShoppingPatronage." *Journal of Economic Psychology* 2, 39-55.

Zimmer, M.R. and L.L. Golden (1988), "Impressions of Retail Stores: A content Analysis of Consumer Images," *Journal of Retailing,* 64(3), 265-293.

Chapter 5

MEASURING THE EFFECT OF DISTANCE ON CONSUMER PATRONAGE BEHAVIOR
a structural equation model and empirical results

1. INTRODUCTION

Store location (or distance) is a factor that influences store choice greatly. Bell et al. (1998) refer to industry research in the US, which indicates that location explains up to 70 percent of the variations in the choice of grocery store (see also Stanley and Sewall, 1976; Verhallen and de Nooij, 1982; Arnold et al., 1983, Nevin and Houston, 1983; Engstrøm and Larsen, 1987; Hortman et al. 1990; Marjanen, 1997; and Levy and Weitz, 2001) for the importance of the location or distance factor in explaining store choice behavior). Eppli (1998) argues however that, over the last couple of decades, the importance of distance may have diminished in explaining consumer store patronage behavior. According to Eppli, the reason for this is that the obstacles of visiting various stores for comparison-shopping have decreased. Large department stores provide a variety of retail goods necessary for comparison-shopping, thus reducing the costs of visiting independent retailers to obtain special commodities. Similarly, in most Western countries, specialty food stores have faced increasing difficulties in competing with supermarkets that are able to offer not only competitive prices, but also a broad assortment of goods as well as convenient shopping (EIU, 1995; Hansen, 2002). Thus, even extensive grocery comparison-shopping could involve just one obstacle for the consumer, i.e., the distance to the preferred warehouse or supermarket.

In line with this discussion, it is likely that the importance of distance will decrease according to how much the consumer feels s/he will achieve, or plans to achieve by visiting a particular store. The distance to the store will probably less influence a consumer who plans to spend a large percentage of her/his housekeeping budgets in a particular store than a consumer who plans to spend only a small percentage of her/his housekeeping budget at the same store. This is due to the fact that the relative use of resource units to cover the distance will be less when the consumer takes care of most of her/his shopping needs than when the consumer only takes care of a small portion of her/his shopping needs. One possible consequence of these reflections is that the importance of distance as a factor in explaining consumers' store choice behavior will probably be influenced by the way in which the actual *measurement* of the consumers' store choice behavior is carried out. If store choice behavior is measured as an expression of the number of times a consumer visits a particular store (frequency), the importance of distance, taking into account the above-mentioned reflections, will presumably be greater than if store choice behavior were to be measured as an expression of the percentage of the housekeeping budget (budget share) spent at a particular store. Frequency (e.g., Marjanen, 1997) as well as budget share (e.g., Hildebrandt, 1988; Solgaard and Hansen, 2001) are frequently used methods of measurement to determine the consumer's store choice behavior. Some researchers (Babin and Attaway, 2000) have combined frequency and budget share with other elements like 'the usual shopping time in a store' into a 'customer share' measure. However, it is difficult to extract a particular pattern regarding the significance of the method of measurement since distance is usually linked with a number of other influential variables, which are not the same for the various published research results which include distance as an influencing variable on consumer store choice behavior. The purpose of this paper is thus to examine the following research proposition more explicitly:

Research Proposition: The significance of distance in explaining the consumer's store choice behavior is influenced by the way in which store choice behavior is construed. The significance of distance will be greater when store choice behavior is measured as the number of times a consumer visits (frequency) a particular store than when store choice behavior is measured as the percentage of housekeeping budget spent (budget share) at a particular store.

The consumers, however, will rarely make a decision based on one piece of information by itself, e.g. information about the distance to the store, rather they will try to collect different pieces of information and determine their behavior on this basis (refer to e.g. Doods et al., 1991; Grewal et al.,

1998). The significance of measuring distance should therefore not be determined by itself, as the significance could relate to other factors, which are regarded as important for the choice of store by the consumer. As stated by Marjanen (1997), "consumers trade off distance with other store-choice variables" (p. 152). Consequently, a conceptual model, which integrates various store choice factors, will be developed in the next section. The model will be developed based on a value perspective of the consumer's store choice behavior. In the following sections, it will form the basis of an empirical survey of a total of eight large Danish supermarket chains. In the final section of the paper, we will be discussing the results of the survey as well as presenting suggestions for further research.

2.   DISTANCE IN A VALUE PERSPECTIVE

Consumer's *perceived value* has been viewed as a strategic and fundamental term for the retail industry (refer to Sweeney and Soutar, 2001). Harnett (1998) believes that retailers capable of offering the consumers 'great value' will be stronger in competition with other retailers. Levy (1999) argues that retail customers are 'value-driven'. Jensen (2001) sees customer value as a "very important concept in marketing strategy" (p. 299). According to Zeithaml (1988), a consumer's perceived value may be seen as an expression of an "overall assessment of the utility of a product (or service) based on perceptions of what is received and what is given" (p. 14). Thus, in principle, the value emerges based partly on what the consumer perceives s/he *receives*, partly on what the consumer perceives s/he *gives*. Within the field of retailing, what the consumer receives may also be termed the store's *service output* (Bucklin, 1966; Stern and El-Ansary, 1988; Bucklin et al., 1996). In order to receive the service output, the consumer must, however, accept a use of certain resources, i.e. a cost. The use of resources may, in this connection, be divided into a use of monetary resources and a use of time resources (refer to e.g., Blackwell et al., 2001). However, both resources are limited, which is why the consumer must try to direct her/his use of resources at the store offering the greatest service output per used resource unit in the eyes of the consumer. From the value perspective point of view, a retailer thus achieves a competitive advantage by offering the consumer greater value than the competitors. In this connection, Gale and Klavans (1985) suggest two different strategies in relation to increasing the consumer's perceived value. One possibility is for the retailer to try to decrease the perceived price and, at the same time, maintain the currently perceived service output. Another possibility is for the retailer to try to improve the perceived service output and, at the same time, maintain the currently perceived price.

The perhaps most common use of the value term relates to the trade-off between quality and price, which may also be termed the 'value-for-money' perspective (e.g. Chang and Wildt, 1994; Monroe, 1990; Abott, 1955; Sweeney et al., 1997; Hansen, 2001; Sweeney and Soutar, 2001). According to Abott (1955), price as well as quality need to be considered when a company wishes to enter a market characterized by competition: "How good a bargain anything is depends upon both quality and price; the two elements *compounded together* form the basis for evaluation of winning contestants in the marketplace" (p. 108). The value term thus encourages the retailer to concentrate both on internal efficiency – low costs – and external efficiency, i.e. creating a quality or, in broader terms, a service output that caters for the wishes and needs of the consumers. From the individual consumer's point of view, the use of the value term means that it is possible to compare the different values of shopping opportunities, and thereby also the individual retailers' ability to satisfy the consumer (Reeves and Bednar, 1994; Teas and Agarwal, 2000). This does not deter some consumers from preferring one particular value package, e.g. the combination of high quality and high price, while others may prefer a value package consisting of the combination of poor quality and low price. Furthermore, some consumers will emphasize price over quality, while others, in turn, will emphasize quality more than price (Zeithaml, 1988).

A value term that refers solely to quality and price would, however, be too restricted a term in relation to the service output that the retailers are able to offer and in relation to the use of resources borne by the consumers (Sweeney and Soutar, 2001; Bolton and Drew, 1991). The service output would also include e.g. assortment (Bucklin et al., 1966), special features or after sales services (Porter, 1990). Furthermore, in choosing a particular store, the consumer is not only burdened with a use of monetary resources in relation to her/his actual purchases, but, among other things, s/he is also burdened with a use of time resources for transportation to and from the physical store. As summarized by Vettas (1999), "consumers make their purchasing decisions after they observe the final 'delivered' prices, that is, prices adjusted for quality plus a transportation cost" (p. 1).

3.   A CONCEPTUAL MODEL

Figure 1 displays the suggested relations between service output, costs and store choice behavior. The assessment of the service output is based on the consumers' own experiences with the three dimensions for each of the retailers. A note about the widespread concept of 'store image' versus 'service output' seems appropriate here.

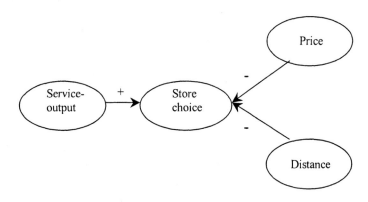

Figure 1. Conceptual model of store choice behavior

Store image is a more comprehensive concept than service output. Store image may be seen as an expression of the store's 'personality' (Martineau, 1958). In general, store image rests on a psychological basis, which may be compared to trait-factor theory (e.g., Buss and Poley, 1976; Haugtvedt et al., 1992). Trait-factor theory is based on the idea that you may attribute individual 'characteristics' to different 'people' (in this connection, different store personalities, brand personalities or similar), which will distinguish them from each other. Store image may (just as brand personality) cover a variety of store perceptions among the consumers concerning concrete matters (e.g. 'low price store'; Finn and Louviere, 1996) as well as the more abstract matters (e.g. 'a strong community reputation'; Arnold et al., 1996). Thus the store image term also refers to factors that are not necessarily direct consequences of a visit to the store in question, but which may also be consequences of the store's social, moral or other societal behavior. In contrast, the term service output solely refers to factors that are dependant on a visit to the store in question (refer to Jensen, 2001). Despite this difference, the many surveys that use the store image terms as their basis may, nevertheless, provide useful information regarding which factors are perceived as significant for choice of store by the consumers when store choice is seen in a service output context.

The literature identifies a number of different dimensions as being potentially significant for the consumer's assessment of individual stores. Mazursky and Jacoby (1985) identified several dimensions that, according to the consumer's perception of the overall image of the store, would affect the choice of store. These dimensions included: merchandise quality, merchandise pricing, merchandise assortment, convenient location, sales clerk service, service in general, store atmosphere, and pleasantness of shopping. In a survey dealing with performance factors in retailing, Hildebrandt (1988) used a total of three dimensions as expressions of store image: quality, atmosphere and price. Bucklin (1966, 1972) specifies service output as comprising the factors, spatial convenience, lot size, waiting or delivery time and product variety. In a survey examining shopping center image and consumer choice behavior, Finn and Louviere (1996) found that two dimensions, wide selection and low prices, could explain 86% of the variation in choice. In a study of consumer attraction to interurban areas, Bell (1999) found a significant relationship between 'quality and range of products and stores' and 'willingness to patronize a retail area'. In a survey of consumers' criteria of choice in choosing between specialty food stores and supermarkets, Hansen (2002) found that the three most important criteria according to the consumers were: high product quality, freshness of products and assortment. Based on the reviewed results, we will assume that the term, service output, is described satisfactorily using the three dimensions: quality, assortment and atmosphere. The model deals with two types of costs: price and distance. Both cost types should be borne by the consumer within her/his usual resource limits. To pay a price to receive a service output involves the use of the consumer's monetary resources, while the distance to the store may involve a use of monetary as well as time resources.

4.   RESEARCH DESIGN

The empirical setting for this research is the Danish supermarket market (refer to Marion, 1998). Various formats constitute the supermarket market in Denmark, namely conventional supermarkets, warehouses, and discount stores. Two large supermarket groups, Dansk Supermarked and FDB, dominate the Danish supermarket market having a marketshare of 68% (2000). The corporate retail chain Dansk Supermarked (marketshare 25%) is owned by Dansk Supermarked Ltd. whereas FDB (marketshare 43%) is a consumer co-op. The Danish independents hold together a marketshare of 28%. Aldi, the German discount store chain, holds a marketshare of 4%. The following stores owned by Dansk Supermarket Ltd. were included in the study: the discount store chain Netto (marketshare 10%), the warehouse chain Bilka (marketshare 5%), and the conventional supermarket chain Føtex (marketshare 10%). The following stores, owned by FDB, were also included in the study: the discount store chain Fakta (marketshare 7%), the warehouse chain Obs (marketshare 3%), and the conventional supermarket chains Kvickly (marketshare 9%) and SuperBrugsen (marketshare 16%). In addition, the discount store chain Aldi was also included in the investigation.

A survey among 631 Danish consumers was performed in order to examine the research proposition. 1500 households were contacted, resulting in a response rate of 42%. The questionnaires were distributed to the respondents by use of the 'drop-off-call-back' method (refer to e.g. Hair et al., 1998). 58 graduate marketing or business students were recruited and trained to serve as data collectors. The training included instructions on how the students were to engage respondents and collect data from them. In order to draw a near balanced proportion of Danish consumers stratified random sampling was used. The students were given instructions as to which area they were to collect data from and were also provided with a signed letter briefly introducing the purpose of the study to the respondents. In addition, students were provided with identity papers. The respondents were approached in their home between 5 p.m. and 8 p.m. If a respondent agreed to participate in the study, the student made an appointment to return for the completed questionnaire (for example one hour later or the next day). The student made sure that the questionnaire had been correctly completed and provided answers to questions, comments, etc. All respondents were promised full confidentiality. When a household consisted of more than one person, the person most often responsible for doing the grocery shopping was chosen as the respondent. For each retail chain, only those respondents who reported that that they were familiar with a particular retail chain and that they use it for grocery shopping at least once in a while, were included in the analyses.

In measuring quality, store atmosphere and price level we choose to follow the suggestions put forward by Hildebrandt (1988) who found that the applied measures confirm both convergent and discriminant validity. Following Hildebrandt, quality, atmosphere and price level was measured by obtaining the respondents response to the following statements: *Quality*: (1) this [retail store chain] offers good quality grocery products; (2) this [retail store chain] offers fresh grocery products. *Atmosphere*: (3) this [retail store chain] has a good in-store atmosphere; (4) this [retail store chain] has a good staff. *Price level*: (5) this [retail store chain] offers low prices; (6) this [retail store chain] has good special offers. In line with these measurements *assortment* was measured by the statements: (7) this [retail store chain] offers a wide selection of grocery products; and (8) this [retail store chain] has frequently new products. All items were measured by a 7-point Likert scale. *Distance* has been measured in a number of ways in various studies. Often, distance has been measured as the physical distance from a subject's residence to an outlet location (e.g., McCarthy, 1980; Hortman et al., 1990). Others (e.g., Cadwallader, 1975; Marjanen, 1997) have used cognitive distance (perceptual distance) as an indicator of distance in combination with other indicators. Still others have considered travelling time and cost distance as important ways of measuring distance (e.g., Saviranta, 1976; Marjanen, 1997). In our study we used the following two measures of distance: (9) What is the typical time distance from your private residence to the [retail store chain] you visit most often? The end-points of the 5-point scale were 'less than 5 minutes' and 'more than 45 minutes', respectively. (10) What is the physical distance from your private residence to the [retail store chain] you visit most often? The end-points of the 7-point scale were 'less than 250 meters' and 'more than 10 kilometers', respectively.

5. RESULTS

The model in Figure 1 was translated into a LISREL model consisting of a measurement part (confirmatory factor analysis) and a structural equation part (simultaneous linear regression). The relationships between the variables were estimated by maximum likelihood estimation.

The results of the measurement model, including the standardized factor loadings, construct reliabilities, and proportion of extracted variance, are displayed in Table 1. All factor loadings were significant ($p<0.01$) which demonstrate that the chosen generic questions for each latent variable reflect a single underlying construct. The reliabilities and variance extracted for each latent variable indicate that the measurement model was reliable and valid. In 44 out of 48 cases construct reliabilities exceed 0.6 (Bagozzi and Yi, 1988). Variance extracted estimates were all above 0.4 with the exception of two cases. The reliabilities and variance were computed using indicator standardized loadings and measurement errors (Hair et al., 1998; Shim et al., 2001).

Relationships were estimated for eight retailers, including three conventional supermarkets, two warehouses, and three discount stores (Table 2). For each retailer two structural equation models were estimated. Model 1 (M1): store choice measured as 'budget share'; Model 2 (M2): store choice measured as 'frequency'.

Table 1. Confirmatory factor analyses results

	Conventional Supermarkets			Warehouses		Discount Stores		
	\multicolumn{8}{c}{Standardized factor loading}							
	R1	R2	R3	R4	R5	R6	R7	Ṙ8
ξ1 Quality								
X1	0.70	0.67	0.81	0.78	0.89	0.80	0.77	0.90
X2	0.70	0.68	0.79	0.88	0.84	0.72	0.87	0.80
ξ2 Assortment								
X3	0.61	0.55	0.73	0.69	0.74	0.63	0.78	0.77
X4	0.65	0.62	0.83	0.76	0.90	0.75	0.60	0.83
ξ3 Atmosphere								
X5	0.69	0.77	0.83	0.78	0.81	0.78	0.81	0.84
X6	0.72	0.69	0.82	0.85	0.81	0.75	0.97	0.77
ξ4 Serviceoutput								
ξ1	0.56	0.65	0.69	0.84	0.81	0.67	0.81	0.81
ξ2	0.67	0.61	0.82	0.74	0.55	0.57	0.68	0.55
ξ3	0.72	0.65	0.79	0.69	0.66	0.62	0.93	0.56
ξ5 Price								
X7	0.82	0.78	0.64	0.75	0.68	0.71	0.82	0.65
X8	0.91	0.84	0.63	0.79	0.74	0.73	0.97	0.70
ξ6 Distance								
X9	0.77	0.72	0.68	0.69	0.72	0.70	0.77	0.71
X10	0.62	0.79	0.62	0.77	0.78	0.63	0.84	0.72
	\multicolumn{8}{c}{Construct reliability}							
	R1	R2	R3	R4	R5	R6	R7	R8
ξ1 Quality	0.66	0.63	0.78	0.82	0.86	0.73	0.81	0.84
ξ2 Assortment	0.57	0.51	0.76	0.69	0.81	0.64	0.65	0.78
ξ3 Atmosphere	0.66	0.70	0.81	0.80	0.79	0.74	0.89	0.79
ξ4 Serviceoutput	0.69	0.67	0.81	0.80	0.72	0.65	0.85	0.68
ξ5 Price	0.85	0.79	0.57	0.74	0.67	0.68	0.89	0.63
ξ6 Distance	0.65	0.73	0.59	0.70	0.72	0.61	0.79	0.68
	\multicolumn{8}{c}{Proportion of extracted variance}							
	R1	R2	R3	R4	R5	R6	R7	R8
ξ1 Quality	0.49	0.46	0.64	0.69	0.75	0.58	0.67	0.73
ξ2 Assortment	0.40	0.34	0.61	0.53	0.68	0.48	0.48	0.64
ξ3 Atmosphere	0.50	0.53	0.68	0.67	0.66	0.59	0.80	0.65
ξ4 Serviceoutput	0.43	0.41	0.59	0.58	0.46	0.39	0.66	0.42
ξ5 Price	0.75	0.66	0.40	0.59	0.51	0.51	0.81	0.46
ξ6 Distance	0.49	0.57	0.42	0.53	0.56	0.44	0.65	0.51

Notes: (A) R1=SuperBrugsen, R2=Føtex, R3=Kvickly, R4=Bilka, R5=Obs, R6=Netto, R7=Aldi, R8=Fakta. (B) The measurement of service output results from a second order factor analysis (refer to e.g. Hair *et al.*, 1998) comprising the variables (items): 'quality', 'assortment', and 'atmosphere'. (C) Store choice is measured by a single item and is therefore not displayed. (D) All factor loadings were significant on the 1% level.

Table 2. Estimates for the proposed model (standardized regression weights)

	Conventional Supermarkets					
	Retailer 1		Retailer 2		Retailer 3	
Relation	M1	M2	M1	M2	M1	M2
SO→Sbeh.	0.44 *	0.18	0.58**	0.47**	0.72**	0.48**
Price→Sbeh.	-0.02	-0.11	-0.19	-0.21	-0.22	-0.11
Distance→Sbeh.	-0.22	-0.70**	-0.54**	-0.71**	-0.59**	-0.71**
n	297		259		167	
χ^2 statistic (p-value)	<0.01	<0.01	<0.01	<0.01	<0.01	<0.01
GFI	0.90	0.91	0.92	0.93	0.90	0.92
Adjusted GFI	0.88	0.87	0.90	0.91	0.87	0.89
CFI	0.90	0.89	0.90	0.92	0.91	0.92
NFI	0.94	0.93	0.93	0.94	0.93	0.93

	Warehouses			
	Retailer 4		Retailer 5	
Relation	M1	M2	M1	M2
SO→Sbeh.	0.73**	0.57**	0.47**	0.42**
Price→Sbeh.	-0.10	-0.16	0.06	0.03
Distance→Sbeh.	-0.57**	-0.70**	-0.51*	-0.71**
n	192		183	
χ^2 statistic (p-value)	<0.01	<0.01	<0.01	<0.01
GFI	0.96	0.91	0.94	0.93
Adjusted GFI	0.92	0.89	0.93	0.92
CFI	0.92	0.93	0.91	0.90
NFI	0.91	0.93	0.92	0.92

	Discount Stores					
	Retailer 6		Retailer 7		Retailer 8	
Relation	M1	M2	M1	M2	M1	M2
SO→Sbeh.	0.39*	0.28	0.51**	0.45**	0.51**	0.32
Price→Sbeh.	-0.59*	-0.43	-0.47*	-0.32	-0.43**	-0.13
Distance→Sbeh.	-0.28	-0.37*	-0.39	-0.51*	-0.43*	-0.68**
n	357		182		179	
χ^2 statistic (p-value)	<0.01	<0.01	<0.01	<0.01	<0.01	<0.01
GFI	0.97	0.92	0.96	0.92	0.94	0.90
Adjusted GFI	0.94	0.89	0.93	0.93	0.92	0.90
CFI	0.98	0.90	0.96	0.90	0.91	0.92
NFI	0.94	0.94	0.93	0.94	0.92	0,93

Notes: (A) Retailer1=SuperBrugsen, Retailer2=Føtex, Retailer3=Kvickly, Retailer4=Bilka, Retailer5=Obs, Retailer6=Netto, Retailer7=Aldi, Retailer8=Fakta. (B) M1 (model 1): Store choice measured as 'budget share'.; M2 (model 2): Store choice measured as 'frequency'. (C) **: Significant on 1% level; *: Significant on 5% level.

This means that a total of 16 models were estimated. The results of the structural equation modeling revealed that the χ^2 for all the estimated models had a p-value <0.01 indicating that the models fail to fit in an absolute sense.

However, several writers (e.g. Hair *et al.*, 1998) recommend that the χ^2 measure should be complemented with other goodness-of-fit measures.

The values of the goodness of fit index (GFI) were all ≥ 0.9, which indicate a good absolute model fit (Bollen and Long, 1993). The values of the adjusted goodness of fit index (AGFI) were in most cases >0.9 and the Bentler and Bonett normed fit index (NFI) showed values >0.9. These values suggest an acceptable improvement of fit over the null model (Drôge, 1989). In addition, the values of the comparative fit index (CFI) were all >0.9. To conclude, acceptable support is provided for the models as proposed.

As can be seen from Table 2 the primary predicting elements of store choice behavior for conventional supermarkets and warehouses were service output and distance. For discount stores the predicting elements include service output, distance as well as price. Except for three cases (retailer1, M2; retailer6, M2; and retailer8, M2), service output had large direct significant effects on store choice behavior. This holds true both when store choice behavior was measured as budget share (M1) and when store choice behavior was measured as frequency (M2). The results also indicate, that our research proposition is supported in the survey. Although distance showed negative effects on store choice behavior when measured as budget share (M1), the negative effects on store choice behavior when measured as frequency (M2) were remarkably larger. We can observe this result for all three categories of retailers, and for all the investigated retail chains. Hence, the results suggest that the significance of distance in explaining consumer store choice behavior is moderated by the actual measurement of store choice behavior. When store choice behavior is measured as 'frequency' the negative effect of distance on store choice behavior is larger than when store choice behavior is measured as 'budget share'.

6. DISCUSSION

The results obtained in this study confirm what has been detected in many studies: distance seems to have a negative effect on consumer store choice behavior. The implication of the present study is, however, that researchers should carefully consider the measurement of store choice behavior when carrying out empirical research involving the concept of distance. The results suggest, that the observed effect of distance on store choice behavior will be influenced by the measurement of store choice behavior. Thus, for all the considered retail chains, the negative effect of distance on store choice behavior when measured as frequency was larger than the negative effect on store choice behavior when measured as budget share. These results have also direct implications for retail managers. In determining the 'right location' for a retail store one may argue, that retail managers should seek the location that offers the highest potential return on investment (refer to Marjanen, 1997). In finding such a location, it is essential that the strategic purpose of the new store is considered. If the strategic purpose is to generate traffic and to attract consumers on a frequently basis, the retail manager should be seriously concerned about the distance to the most wanted customers and may thus consider an in-town location (Guy, 1994). Otherwise, if the strategic purpose is to attract consumers conducting extensive grocery shopping, the retail manager may consider locations in out of town areas. However, in determining the right location a number of other aspects need also to be taken into consideration. For example, it is probably more costly for a low quality retailer (e.g. a discount store) than for a high quality retailer (e.g. an up-scale conventional supermarket) to locate near its rivals (Vettas, 1999). A low quality retailer may prefer to move away in competitive space in an effort to reduce price competition. In contrast, a retailer which posses a large quality advantage may seek to enjoy this advantage by moving closer to its rivals (Vettas, 1999). Also, the high quality retailer may wish to provide information to consumers that help them to compare the quality of the products offered by competitive retailers. This may further help consumers to evaluate the offered value and, at the same time, it may urge consumers to put less weight on price when making assessments of value (refer to Lynch & Ariely, 2000). In incidents, where consumers are faced with high uncertainty when making judgments of the quality of the offered products, a retailer's location can be used by consumers as a signal of quality (Richardson et al., 1994; Vettas, 1999). However, a low quality retailer seeking to exploit this opportunity face the risk of disappointing the consumers, which may prevent them from repeat shopping in that particular store.

An emerging competitive threat to nearly all retailing segments is the Internet (Rigby, 1998; Sheth et al., 2001). With a very few exceptions Danish grocery retailers have not yet on any significant scale gone into internet trading because for most retailers, there is not yet a profitable format for using the internet. However, Internet trading could certainly be expected to intensify future retail competition and to influence retail location planning. According to The Economist (1995), "the death of distance as a determinant of the cost of communications will probably be the single most important economic force shaping society...it will alter, in ways that are only imaginable, decisions about were people live and work; concepts of national borders; patterns of international trade" (p. 39).

This research is limited in that it does not consider a wide range of factors, which potentially may affect consumer store choice behavior. Thus, we do not propose that we have 'fully explained' consumer store choice behavior. At the same time, such an explanation has not been the purpose of the present study. Instead, emphasis has been put on the significance of distance in combination with different measurements of store choice behavior. In addressing this problem setting, future research may wish to combine other predicting variables of store choice behavior (e.g., perceived hedonic and utilitarian shopping value, accessibility of the stores, *etc.*) with distance. Also, potentially moderating variables like available modes of transportation, income, age and other socioeconomic factors, and psychological factors as e.g. attitudes and interests may be taken into account.

7. CONCLUSION

This study addressed the influence of distance on store choice behavior when store choice behavior was measured in different ways. On the basis of a structural equation model involving service output, price and distance it was found that the negative effect of distance on store choice behavior was remarkably larger when store choice behavior was measured as 'frequency' than when store choice behavior was measured as 'budget share'. This result was consistent across all the investigated categories of retailers, i.e., conventional supermarkets, warehouses and discount stores.

REFERENCES

Abbott, L.: *Quality and Competition*, Columbia University Press, New York (1955).

Arnold, S.J., Oum, T.H., and Tigert, D.J.: Determinant attributes in retail patronage: seasonel, temporal and international comparisons, *Journal of Marketing Research*, 20 (1983): 146-157.

Arnold, S.J., Handelman, J., and Tigert, D.J.: Organizational Legitimacy and Retail Store Patronage, *Journal of Business Research*, 35 (1996): 229-239.

Babin, B.J., and Attaway, J.S.: Atmospheric Affect as a Tool for Creating Value and Gaining Share of Customer, *Journal of Business Research*, 49 (2000), 91-99.

Bagozzi, R.P., and Yi, Y.: On the Evaluation of Structural Equation Models, *Journal of the Academy of Marketing Science*, Vol. 16, No. 1 (1988): 74-94.

Bell, D.R., Ho, T-J., and Tang, C.S.: Determining Where to Shop: Fixed and Variable Costs of Shopping, *Journal of Marketing Research*, 35 (1998): 352-369.

Bell, S.J.: Image and consumer attraction to interurban retail areas: An environmental psychology approach, *Journal of Retailing and Consumer Services*, 6 (1999): 67-78.

Blackwell, R.D., Miniard, P.W., and Engel, J.F.: *Consumer Behavior*, Harcourt Publications, ninth edition (2001).

Bollen, K.A. and Long, J.S.: *Testing Structural Equation Models*, London SAGE Publications (1993).

Bolton, R.N. and Drew, J.H.: A Multistage Model of Customers' Assessments of Service Quality and Value, *Journal of Consumer Research*, 17 (March) (1991): 375-384.

Bucklin, L.P.: *A theory of distribution channel structure*, Institute of Business and Economic Research, Berkeley, CA. (1966).

Bucklin, L.P.: *Competition and Evolution of in the Distributive Trades*, Prentice-Hall N.J. (1972)

Bucklin, L.P., Ramaswamy, V., and Majumdar, S.K.: Analyzing channel structures of business markets via the Structure-Output Paradigm, *International Journal of Research in Marketing*, 13 (1996): 73-87.

Buss, A.R. and Poley, W.: *Individual Differences: Traits and Factors*, Halsted Press: New York (1976).

Cadwallader, M.: A behavioral model of consumer spatial decision making, *Economic Geography*, 51 (1975): 339-349.

Chang, T-Z. and Wildt, A.R.: Price, product information, and purchase intention; An empirical study, *Journal of the Academy of Marketing Science*, Vol. 22 (1994): 16-27.

Dodds, W.B., Monroe, K.B., and Grewal, D.: The Effects of Price, Brand, and Store Information on Buyers' Products Evaluations, *Journal of Marketing Research*, 28 (August 1991): 307-319.

Drôge, C.: Shaping the Route to Attitude Change: Central versus Peripheral Processing Through Comparative versus Noncomparative Advertising, *Journal of Marketing Research*, Vol. XXVI (May) (1989): 193-204.

EIU, The Economist Intelligence Unit Limited: Specialist food shops, *Retail Trade Review*, No. 36 (1995).

Engstrøm, H. and Larsen, H.H.: *Husholdningernes Butiksvalg: Indkøbsadfærd for Dagligvarer*, Nyt Nordisk Forlag, Copenhagen (1987).

Eppli, M.J.: Value Allocation in Regional Shopping Centers, *The Appraisal Journal*, April (1998): 198-206.

Finn, A. and Louviere, J.J.: Shopping Center Image, Consideration, and Choice: Anchor Store Contribution, *Journal of Business Research*, 35 (1996): 241-251.

Gale, B.T. and Klavans, R.: Formulating a Quality Improvement Strategy
The Journal of Business Strategy, Vol. 5, Iss. 3 (1985): 21-31.

Grewal, D., Monroe, K.B., and Krishnan, R.: The effects of price-comparison advertising on buyers' perceptions of acquisition value, transaction value, and behavioral intentions, *Journal of Marketing*, Vol. 62, Iss. 2 (1998): 46-59.

Guy, C.: *The Retail Development Process – location, property and planning*, Routledge, London.

Hair, J., Anderson, R.E., Tatham, R.L., and Black, W.C.: *Multivariate Data Analysis*, Fifth ed., Prentice-Hall, New Jersey (1998).

Hansen, T.: Quality in the Marketplace: A Theoretical and Empirical Investigation, *European Management Journal*, Vol. 19 (2001): 203-211.

Hansen, T.: Intertype Competition: Specialty Food Stores Competing with Supermarkets, *Journal of Retailing and Consumer Services*, Vol. 10(1) (2003): 35-49.

Harnett, M.: Shopper Needs Must Be Priority, *Discount Store News*, 37 (1998): 21-22.

Haugtvedt, C., Petty, R.E., and Cacioppo, J.T.: Need for Cognition and Advertising: Understanding the Role of Personality Variables in Consumer Behavior, *Journal of Consumer Psychology*, 1 (1992): 239-260.

Hildebrandt, L.: Store Image and the Prediction of Performance in Retailing, *Journal of Business Research*, 17 (1988): 91-100.

Hortman, S.M., Allaway, A.W., Mason, J.B., and Rasp, J.: Multisegment Analysis of Supermarket Patronage, *Journal of Business Research*, 21 (1990): 209-223.

Jensen, H.R.: Antecedents and consequences of consumer value assessments: implications for marketing strategy and future research, *Journal of Retailing and Consumer Services*, 8 (2001): 299-310.

Levy, M.: Revolutionizing the Retail Pricing Game, *Discount Store News*, 38 (1999): 15.

Levy, M., and Weitz, B.A.: *Retailing Management*, McGraw-Hill Irwin, (2001): Fourth Edition.

Lynch Jr., J.G. & Ariely, D.: Wine Online: Search Costs and Competition on Price, Quality, and Distribution, *Marketing Science*, Vol. 19(1) (2001).

Marion, B.W.: Competition in grocery retailing: the impact of a new strategic group on BLS price increases, *Review of Industrial Organization*, 13 (1998): 381-399.

Marjanen, H.: *Distance and Store Choice*, Publications of the Turku School of Economics and Business Administration, Series A-4 (1997).

Martineau, P.D.: The Personality of the Retail Store, *Harvard Business Review*, 36 (January-February 1958): 47-55.

Mazursky, D. and Jacoby, J.: Exploring the Development of Store Images, *Journal of Retailing*, 62 (1985): 145-165.

McCarthy, P.S.: A study of the importance of generalized attributes in shopping choice behavior, *Environment and Planning A*, Vol. 12 (1980): 1269-1286.

Monroe, K.B.: *Pricing: Making Better Profitable Decisions*, McGraw-Hill: New York, 2nd edition (1990).

Nevin, J.R., and Houston, M.J.: Image as a Component of Attraction to Interurban Shopping Areas, *Journal of Retailing*, Vol. 56 (Spring) (1983): 77-93.

Porter, M.E.: *The competitive advantage of nations*, New York: MacMillan Press (1990).

Reeves, C.A. and Bednar, D.A.: Defining Quality: alternatives and implications, *Academy of Management Review*, Vol. 19, No. 3 (1994): 419-445.

Richardson, P.S., Dick, A.S., and Jain, A.K.: Extrinsic and Intrinsic Cue Effects on Perceptions of Store Brand Quality, *Journal of Marketing*, Vol. 58 (1994): 28-36.

Rigby, P.E.: Trends in retailing, *Commercial Lending Review*, 13 (1) (1998): 7-9.

Saviranta, J.: Perception of the friction caused by distance in shopping trips, *The Finnish Journal of Business Economics*, 3 (1976): 378-397.

Sheth, J.N., Eshghi, A., and Krishnan, B.C.: *Internet Marketing*, Harcourt College Publishers, New York (2001).

Shim, S., Eastlick, M.A., Lotz, S.L., and Warrington, P.: An online prepurchase intentions model: The role of intention to search, *Journal of Retailing*, 77 (2001): 397-416.

Solgaard, H.S. and Hansen, T.: A Hierarchical Bayes Model of Store Choice: Modeling Choice Between Discount Stores, Hypermarkets and Conventional Supermarkets, Working Paper, Department of Marketing, Copenhagen Business School (2001).

Stanley, T.J., and Sewall, M.A.: Image Inputs to a Probabilistic Model: Predicting Retail Potential, *Journal of Marketing*, Vol. 40 (July) (1976): 48-53.

Stern, L.W. and El-Ansary, A.I.: *Marketing Channels*, Englewood Cliffs, NJ, Prentice-Hall, Inc. (1988).

Sweeney, J.C., and Soutar, G.N.: Consumer perceived value: The development of a multiple item scale, *Journal of Retailing*, 77 (2001): 203-220.

Teas, K.R. and Agarwal, S.: The Effects of Intrisinc Product Cues on Consumers' Perceptions of Quality, Sacrifice, and Value, *Journal of the Academy of Marketing Science*, Vol. 28, No. 2 (2000): 278-290.

The Economist: The Death of Distance, 30 September (1995): 39.

Verhallen, T.M.M. and de Nooij, G.J.: Retail Attribute Sensitivity and Shopping Patronage, *Journal of Economic Psychology*, 2 (1982): 39-55.

Vettas, N.: *Location as a Signal of Quality*, Discussion Paper Series, No. 2165, Centre for Economic Policy Research, London (1999).

Zeithaml, V.A.: Consumer Perceptions of Price, Quality, and Value: A Means-End Model and Synthesis of Evidence, *Journal of Marketing*, Vol. 52 (1988): 2-22.

Chapter 6

INTERTYPE COMPETITION[*]
specialty food stores competing with supermarkets

1.   INTRODUCTION

The development of competitive advantage is one of the main challenges which food stores is facing. In fact, retailing in general has been regarded as one of the most dynamic and competitive areas of business organization (Collins, 1992; Leszczyc et al., 2000). While food is essential to life consumers cannot consume unlimited amounts of food. Facing a near-saturated market, being the case in most Western countries, retailers seek to find ways to differentiate themselves from other retailers and thereby creating preference, or even loyalty, towards their own outlets. In short, retailers are aiming for competitive advantages. A competitive advantage can be defined as "a unique position which a firm develops vis-á-vis its competitors through its patterns of resource deployments and/or scope of decisions" (Hofer & Schendel, 1978, p. 25). A retailer obtains a competitive advantage by offering consumers a considerable 'service-output' at a given cost, as compared to competing retailers. Two types of competitive interaction among retailers are most commonly identified (Ingene, 1983; Miller, 1999; Levy and Weitz, 2001): (1) *Intratype competition*, which refers to competition between the *same* type of outlets (e.g., a specialty food store competing with another specialty food store). (2) *Intertype competition*, which refers to competition between *different* types of outlets (e.g., a

[*] Reprinted from Journal of Retailing and Consumer Services, Vol. 10, Hansen, Torben, Intertype competition: specialty food stores competing with supermarkets, pp. 35-49, Copyright (2003), with permission from Elsevier Science.

specialty food store competing with a supermarket). This paper deals with the second type of competition. The purpose of the paper is to investigate how specialty food stores compete with supermarkets. Towards this end, we consider the following problem areas: Are there correspondence between the importance assigned by specialty food store managers and consumers to various store choice factors (Baker and Hart, 1989; Hildebrandt, 1988); what are managers' intended image of specialty food stores and what is the image as perceived by consumers; and how competitive are specialty food stores in future intertype competition with supermarkets?

The purpose of this study is approached from both a specialty food store-oriented perspective and a consumer-oriented perspective: The total service-output of a specialty food store would include factors such as the location of the shop, information about the shop and its products, assortment, customization of products, product quality, *etc.* None of these, or other factors, should be excluded beforehand as having potential for gaining 'competitive advantages'. The competitiveness of specialty food stores when participating in intertype competition with supermarkets can therefore be regarded as an abstract concept, which in itself does not provide much information about the critical success factors of specialty food stores. Instead, a distillation of the concept has to be made in order to provide more specific information about the factors which specialty food stores consider as being important for their competitiveness. However, whether the perceived critical success factors of specialty food store managers are sufficient for competing in the food market depends highly on the importance attached by consumers to these critical factors when choosing among different types of food-outlets. In consequence of these considerations, two quantitative studies were conducted. The first study elicits specialty food store managers' opinions of their critical success factors and of their estimated future competiveness when competing with supermarkets. This study encompasses four types of specialty food stores. The second study elicits consumers' assessments of the most important store choice factors when deciding whether to choose a specialty food store or a supermarket.

This paper takes its point of departure in Danish retailing. The historical development in Danish retailing has in general terms been close to the historical development in the rest of the Western countries. Like in most other Western countries there has been a decrease in the number of food outlets complemented by a larger geographical and economical concentration of retailers. The results obtained in this study might therefore also be of interest to retailers and academics in other Western countries. This paper is organized as follows: In section 2, a review of the present intertype competitive position of specialty food stores is conducted. Also, an overview of the Danish food retail structure is provided. In section 3, four research questions are established, as is the methodology used. The results of the two empirical studies are presented in section 4. Section 5 discusses the implications of the obtained results and provides suggestions for further research. In section 6 some concluding remarks are proposed.

2.   THE COMPETITIVE CONTEXT

According to Porter (1979, p. 215) "an industry can...be viewed as composed of clusters or groups of firms, where each group consists of firms following similar strategies in terms of key decision variables...I define such groups as *strategic groups*". The Danish retail food market can be divided into six strategic groups each offering a unique mix of price, service, and products. Three of these strategic groups - warehouses, discount supermarkets, and conventional supermarkets - compete for the major shopping trips of consumers and can together be labeled the 'supermarket market' (see Marion, 1998). Other three strategic groups - minimarkets, specialty food stores, and kiosks - compete for fill-in or specialty shopping. These three groups can together be labeled the 'fill-in market' (see Marion, 1998). Although the supermarket market and the fill-in market represent two different ways of distributing food to consumers they both compete for the consumers' food money. In this paper the widest possible definition of a 'supermarket' is used covering the 'supermarket market'. With regards to the fill-in market this paper is focusing on specialty food stores only. A specialty store is usually defined as "a small or medium-sized establishment or boutique handling limited lines of goods" (Stern & El-Ansary, 1988, p. 42).

2.1   The Danish supermarket market and specialty food stores

Various formats constitute the supermarket market in Denmark, namely discount stores, warehouses (i.e. hypermarkets and combination stores), and conventional supermarkets (including up-scale supermarkets). Two large supermarket groups, Dansk Supermarked and FDB, dominate the Danish supermarket market having a total marketshare of 68% (2000). The corporate retail chain Dansk Supermarked (marketshare 25%) is owned by Dansk Supermarked Ltd. whereas FDB (marketshare 43%) is a consumer co-op. The Danish independents hold together a marketshare of 28%. 55% of the independents are joined in wholesale-sponsored voluntary cooperative groups whereas 32% are joined in retail-sponsored cooperatives (refer to Levy & Weitz, 2001). Aldi, the German discount store chain, holds a marketshare of 4% of the supermarket market.

Dansk Supermarked comprises the discount store chain Netto (marketshare 10%), the hypermarket chain Bilka (marketshare 5%), and the combination store chain Føtex (marketshare 10%). FDB comprises the discount store chain Fakta (marketshare 7%), the hypermarket chain OBS (marketshare 3%), the combination store chain Kvickly (marketshare 9%), the conventional supermarket chains SuperBrugsen (marketshare 16%) and Dagli'Brugsen (marketshare 5%), and the up-scale chain Irma (marketshare 2%). The Danish independents comprise conventional supermarkets (total marketshare 22%), discount supermarkets (total marketshare of 4%) and others (total marketshare 2%). In general, Danish specialty food stores can be characterized as owner managed independents, since cooperation and integration among these stores is almost absent (MBI, 2000; Stockmann, 2000). There are a total of 5700 (2000) specialty food stores in Denmark, which together hold a marketshare of 45% of the fill-in food market and about 12% of the total food market.

2.2   The changing Danish food retail structure

The retail structure in Denmark, as well as in other Western countries, has undergone some remarkable changes over the last couple of decades. Since 1970 the number of specialty food stores in Denmark has declined dramatically (Table 1).

Table 1. The number of selected specialty food stores in Denmark[a]

	1970	1980	1993	1995	1997	2000
Greengrocer's shops	3.781	1.527	920	822	748	728
Butcher's shops	4.313	2.402	1.053	951	877	853
Baker's shops	3.755	2.594	1.605	1.465	1.368	1.092
Cheese-shops	551	357	201	181	168	149

[a]*Source*: The Danish Statistical Bureau (1985, 2000).

Also, the total number of food retailers in the Danish marketplace has been declining over the last couple of decades. In the period from 1982 to 1992 the number of grocery retailers in Europe has been reduced by 17%. In comparison, the number of grocery retailers in Denmark has been reduced by 37% in the period from 1982 to 1992, which is a much larger reduction (Larsen, 1996). In the more extensive period from 1970 to 2000 the number of supermarkets has been reduced by 65% and in the same period the number of specialty food stores has been reduced by 73%. Also a number of others factors are relevant to emphasize.

1. The number of supermarket square meters has in the period from 1975 to 2000 grown by more than 95%.

2. There has been an increase in the *economic concentration* among the supermarkets. In 1988 the two largest Danish supermarket groups, FDB and Dansk Supermarked, had together a marketshare of 49% of the supermarket market. In 2000 their total marketshare has increased to 68%. Also the *geographic concentration* has increased remarkable during the last decades. Many small grocery stores have withdrawn from the marketplace, first of all due to a lack of ability to compete on low costs and assortment (MBI, 2000). However, in spite of this the density of grocery stores is still among the highest in Northern Europe, which leaves potential room for further integration and economic rationalization.
3. In the period 1990 to 2000 total Danish private consumption has grown by 27%. However, in the same period, total Danish consumption of grocery has only grown by 7% which implies a much smaller market growth compared to the growth of branches like tourism, entertainment, transportation *etc.*, which each has grown by well over 20%.
4. In 1980 there were only 16 discount supermarkets present in the Danish marketplace. In 2001 this number has gone up to 855.
5. An emerging competitive threat to nearly all retailing segments is the Internet (Rigby, 1998; Sheth et al., 2001). With a very few exceptions Danish grocery retailers have not yet on any significant scale gone into internet trading because for most retailers, there is not yet a profitable format for using the internet. However, Internet trading could certainly be expected to intensify future retail competition.

2.3   The intertype competitiveness of specialty food stores

The declining number of specialty food stores does not in itself say anything about the relative competitiveness of the stores since the number of supermarkets has been declining almost as dramatically (see Table 2). Therefore, a more accurate measure of the relative competitive strength has to be applied. In a study of restaurants versus grocery stores Ingene (1983) suggests that the proportion of restaurant sales is indicative of the relative, competitive strength of restaurants. Following Ingene, a measure of intertype competition can be calculated as the proportion of supermarket plus specialty food store sales accounted for by specialty food stores alone. The results of applying this measure are also displayed in Table 2. From Table 2 it can be seen that the proportion of total food sales accounted for by specialty food stores has decreased by almost 68% since 1970 (from 42.9% to 13.8%). This indicates that the relative, competitive strength of specialty food stores has been declining substantially over the years. The same picture appears when the per specialty food store proportion of food sales is calculated. This proportion has declined to an almost similar degree (by 64%).

Table 2. Intertype competition displayed[a]

	1970	1980	1990	2000
Number of supermarkets	12.400	7.800	6.000	4.300
Number of specialty food stores	21.000	11.000	6.600	5.700
Proportion of specialty food stores (%)	62.9	58.5	52.4	57.0
Supermarket food sales (bill. dkk.) (1)	8	28	47	69
Specialty food store sales (bill dkk.)	6	8	10	11
Proportion of total sales acc. for by spec. f. stores	42.9	22.2	17.5	13.8
Food sales per supermarket (1000 dkk.)	645	3.589	7.833	16.046
Food sales per spec. food store (1000 dkk.)	286	727	1.515	1.930
Proportion of food sales per spec. f. store (%)	30.1	16.8	16.2	10.7
Gross profit in percentage of total sales				
Supermarkets		16(2)	18	19(3)
Specialty food stores		29(2)	29	33(3)

Notes: (1) The supermarket sales figures amount to 60% of total sales which are the estimated average sales originated in food alone (Stockmann, 1999, 2000).
(2) 1982-figures. (3) 1997-figures.
[a]*Sources:* The Danish Statistical Bureau (1985, 2000); Stockmann (2000); MBI (2000).

However, it will also be noted from Table 2 that the gross profit ratio originated in food sales has slightly increased since 1980 for both supermarkets (+19%) and specialty food stores (+14%). This indicates that the *remaining* specialty food stores are performing quite well and that they, so far, have been able to adapt themselves to the remarkable changes in the Danish food retailing structure. As emphasized in the introduction, the question is, however, whether this tendency will be continued in future retailing or whether the numbers of specialty food stores will still be declining.

2.4   Summary

The changes that over the last couple of decades have taken place in the Danish food retail structure may be summarized as follows:

- A dramatic closure of specialty food stores
- A dramatic decrease in the marketshare obtained by specialty food stores in the Danish retail food market
- A steady rise in the average store size

- A successful introduction of discount supermarkets
- A higher concentration level
- Both supermarkets and specialty food stores have managed to increase their gross profit ratio.

3. RESEARCH QUESTIONS AND METHODOLOGY

3.1 Research questions

Based on the results from the previous section and a literature review of retail competition factors and retail store patronage, four research questions (RQ's) are established in the following:

Specialty food store managers' evaluation of critical success factors (RQ1): In general, the term 'success factor' is taken for "key variables that are empirically related to an indicator of performance (e.g., return on investment, return on assets)" (Hildebrandt, 1988, p. 92). Rockart (1979) argues that critical success factors are those factors, which may result in successful competitive performance for an organization. Urbany et al. (2000) state that retail grocery executives apply promotion activities for the primary effect of "stealing traffic from competitors' stores" (p. 243). Arnold et al. (1996) found that "retailer action on attributes such as price, value for money, locational convenience, etc., determines store choice" (p. 237). Making priorities to different combinations of store factors may therefore have a direct influence on store performance (refer to Wilcox & O'Callaghan, 2001) and competitiveness. The process of making priorities must reflect and respond to changes in retail structure and must take into account possible changes in consumers preference structures (Arnold et al., 1998). Thus, specialty food store managers should continuously monitor their critical success factors in order to make necessary adjustments if needed:

RQ1: Which factors are considered by specialty food store managers to be the most critical when participating in intertype competition with supermarkets?

The importance assigned by consumers to store choice factors (RQ2): In the store patronage literature (e.g. Arnold et al., 1998; Sirgy et al., 2000) it is suggested that consumers decide on a number of store factors among which some of them may be determinant in the patronage decision. In this connection, it is a vital step for being competitive that specialty food store managers' and consumers' assigned importance to the store factors correspond. An inconsistency between specialty food stores and consumers on this matter could easily lead to the two parties 'passing each other by' in the marketplace. For example, it will hardly have any competitive effect for a food store to try to improve its 'in-store cleaning' if consumers do not assign importance to that factor. Research has observed that managers often misestimate consumer preference for both price and nonprice product or service factors. In a study of 92 store managers and 422 consumers Urbany et al. (2000) found that managers tend to overestimate aggregate price comparison behavior and cross-store shopping. Additionally, it was found that managers simultaneously underestimate consumer newspaper readership, in-store search for specials, and stockpilling. In another (however limited) study of 12 executives Urbany et al. (1991) found that retail grocery executives substantially overestimate price promotion response when compared to consumers' self-reports. Based on several in-depth interviews with managers and focus group interviews with consumers Parasuraman et al. (1985) argue that "executives may not always understand what features a service must have in order to meet consumer needs" (p. 44). Such evidence suggests, that insight into consumers' assigned importance to various store choice factors should be achieved:

> RQ2: Which factors are considered by consumers to be the most critical when deciding whether to choose a specialty food store instead of a supermarket? Do these factors correspond to specialty food store managers' evaluation of critical success factors?

Consumers' perception of specialty food store image (RQ3): Consumers are frequently faced with judging the quality of food, when determining what brand to buy, in what amount. Many food products are, however, extremely complex and the consumer may neither have the time nor the motivation to engage in comparative evaluations of brands prior to purchase. Moreover, it may be difficult for consumers to assess the importance of various quality-aspects in relation to each other and in relation to requirements rooted in the intended use of the product (SOU, 1994; Steenkamp, 1989). Therefore consumers are often faced with uncertainty when making judgments of the quality of food products. According to Bell (1999) consumers who face difficulties in evaluating a product or a store may use their perceptions of store image as a proxy for the quality of the goods provided. Store image is based upon the consumers' perception of a number of salient store factors (refer to Hildebrandt, 1988) e.g. high service level, friendly workers, and fair prices. Considerable research has been devoted to the conceptual and empirical aspects of store image and its role in explaining store patronage behavior. Martineau (1958) suggested as one of the first that a store's image influences shopping behavior. Hildebrandt (1988) found a slightly negative effect of low-price image on consumer budget spending in specialty food stores. Arnold et al. (1996) found that if a retailer is being identified as having a 'strong community reputation' it may not only affect store choice but also moderate the effect of other factors like e.g. price. In a study of shopping center image and consumer choice behavior Finn and Louviere (1996) report that two image items ('wide selection' and 'low prices') accounted for 86% of the variance in share of choice. In a recent study of image and consumer attraction to interurban retail areas Bell (1999) found significant relationships between 'quality and range of products and stores', 'visual amenity' and consumers' willingness to patronize a retail area. Based on the discussion above, an analysis of the intertype competitiveness of specialty food stores should also address the following question:

RQ3: What is the image of specialty food stores as perceived by consumers, and does this image correspond to specialty food store managers' intended store image?

Future intertype competitiveness of specialty food stores (RQ4): The research questions established so far only represent an evaluation of the present situation and do not say much about the *future* intertype competitiveness of specialty food stores. Thus, a complementary research question is formulated:

RQ4: What is the estimated future intertype competitiveness of specialty food stores?

3.2   Data collection and setting

Two surveys were performed in order to provide answers to the research questions. Study 1 consists of 161 respondents (specialty food store managers) from all regions of Denmark. Nine hundred and sixty survey questionnaires were mailed out for this mail survey study resulting in a response rate of 16.8%. Stratified random sampling was utilized in order to draw a near balanced proportion of stores in accordance with their respective population. Specifically, 26% of the sample was drawn among greengrocer's shops, 20% among butcher's shops, 43% among baker's shops, and the remaining 10% among cheese-shops. The respondents were promised complete confidentiality and were instructed to return the questionnaires to the university where this study was conducted. A self-addressed stamped return envelope was provided. Study 2 consists of 631 Danish consumers.

1500 households were contacted resulting in a response rate of 42%. The questionnaires were distributed to the respondents by use of the 'drop-off-call-back' method (refer to e.g. Hair *et al.*, 2000). 58 graduate marketing or business students were recruited and trained to serve as data collectors in study 2. The training included instructions to the students on how they were to engage respondents and collect data from them. In order to draw a near balanced proportion of Danish consumers stratified random sampling was utilized. The students were given instructions on in which area they were to collect data and were also provided with a signed letter, which briefly introduced the purpose of the study to the respondents. In addition, students were provided with identity papers. The respondents were approached at their home in the period from 5 p.m. to 8 p.m. If a respondent agreed to participate the student made an appointment on when to return for the completed questionnaire (for example one hour later or the next day). The student made sure that the questionnaire was correctly completed and gave answers to questions, comments, etc. All respondents were promised complete confidentiality. When a household consisted of more than one person the person most often responsible for doing the food-shopping was chosen as the respondent.

It was very important that the theoretical concepts used in study 1 and 2 (e.g., success factors, choice factors, and competitiveness) and their implementation was in agreement. It was also of great importance that these implementations were perceived by the respondents as deliberate. The following procedures were used in order to ensure this (Bagozzi, 1994): (1) A preliminary first draft was prepared. (2) The draft was subsequently assessed by four researchers competent in retail competitiveness and store patronize behavior. The draft was also assessed by five non-experts. This step resulted in a number of adjustments. (3) Following these adjustments, the questions were shown to two more experts and three non-experts. This step resulted in minor corrections only. (4) Finally a pre-test was carried out (five experts and five non-experts). This test did only result in a very few further adjustments of the measurements used.

3.3   Measurements

The opinion of specialty food store managers concerning their critical success factors were measured in study 1. A 7-point semantic scale with end-points 'not very important' and 'very important' for competing with supermarkets was applied. Specialty food store managers were asked to assign their perceived importance towards 29 competition factors. The selection of the factors was made on basis of a comprehensive review of the existing literature concerning competition and specialty food stores as well as consumer store choice behavior (e.g., Hise et al., 1983; Mazursky and Jacoby, 1986; Hildebrandt, 1988; Arnold et al., 1998; Bell, 1999).

The importance assigned by consumers to store choice factors was measured in study 2. A 7-point semantic scale with end-points 'not very important' and 'very important' for choosing a specialty food store instead of a supermarket was applied. Consumers were asked to assign their perceived importance towards 25 store choice factors. Naturally, most of the store choice factors were identical with the competition factors. However, some of the competition factors (competence of management, reliability of supplier delivery, good atmosphere among workers, customer loyalty, and discounts from suppliers) were internal factors (Bamberger, 1989), which cannot be perceived by consumers. Only specialty food store managers have therefore been asked to evaluate the importance of these factors. Similar, some consumers may choose a specialty food store when shopping for a 'special occasion'. But consumers' 'special occasions' are not among those factors, which can be directly manipulated by specialty food store managers. Thus, only consumers have been asked to evaluate the importance of this factor.

For the purpose of measuring consumers' perceived image of specialty food stores the 25 store choice factors measured in study 2 were reduced into a fewer dimensions by the use of principal-component analysis. The dimensions where then included as independent variables in a multiple regression analysis with 'shopping frequency' as the dependent variable. A more thoroughly explanation of this measurement method is provided in paragraph 4.3.

Future intertype competitiveness was measured in study 1 by three different measurements: Measurement 1 measured specialty store manager's response to the following statement: "Compared to the competitiveness of the nearest supermarket, how would you describe *your* overall future level of competitiveness?" Measurement 1 was measured on a 7-point semantic scale with end-points 'much worser' and 'much better' respectively. In measurement 2 the level of perceived competitiveness was measured by a two-item scale. The first item measured the manager's response to the following statement: "Compared to the ability of the nearest supermarket, how would you describe *your* ability to attract new customers?" The second item measured the manager's response to the statement: "Compared to the ability of the nearest supermarket, how would you describe *your* ability to hold on to existing customers?" Both items were measured on a 7-point semantic scale with end-points 'much worser' and 'much better' respectively. A third measurement of future perceived competitiveness was obtained by applying the formula:

$$\text{Competitiveness} = \sum_{i,j,k=1}^{n} B_{ijk}I_{ik}$$

where i is the competition factor, j the specialty store, k the specialty store manager, B the specialty store manager k's belief regarding the extent to which specialty store j possesses competition factor i, I the importance weight given to future competition factor i by specialty store manager k.

In this formula competitiveness is based on the summed set of beliefs held by specialty store manager k that specialty store j possesses competition factor i multiplied by the importance given to future competition factor i by specialty store manager k.

4.   RESULTS

4.1   Research question 1: Specialty food store managers' evaluation of critical success factors

Table 3 displays two set of factors: (a) the importance given by specialty food store managers to a number of intertype competition factors; (b) the importance given by consumers to a number of store choice factors. In this paragraph only the factors in column (a) are examined.

As can be seen from Table 3 specialty store managers rate high product quality (scored 6.92 on the applied 7-point scale) and freshness of products (scored 6.91) as the two most important factors for competing with supermarkets. According to specialty food store managers a good reputation is not achieved by applying direct mail (scored 2.90, ranked 28) or advertising in newspapers or magazines (scored 3.32, ranked 25). This indicates, that mainly word-of-mouth communication is perceived by managers as important for gaining a good reputation.

This result is consistent with other previous studies (e.g., Engel *et al.*, 1969; Myers & Robertson, 1972) which show that advertising is probably more effective at creating awareness and at reinforcing existing preferences than at creating new ones (e.g., Solomon *et al.*, 1999; Martilla, 1971). One of the strength of a supermarket is that it offers a wide variety of different food categories. But by offering all these categories it is difficult to have a great depth of assortment within every product category.

Table 3. Critical factors for competing with supermarkets

	(a) Specialty store manager opinion			(b) Customer opinion		
	Importance			Importance		
	SD	Mean	Rank	Rank	Mean	SD
High product quality	0.35	6.92	1	2	6.11	1.32
Freshness of products	0.42	6.91	2	1	6.14	1.25
A good reputation	0.52	6.81	3	11	5.00	1.82
Friendly workers	0.54	6.77	4	8	5.47	1.58
High service level	0.55	6.76	5	4	5.60	1.52
In-store cleaning	0.72	6.75	6	6	5.55	1.52
Good in-store atmosphere	0.78	6.60	7	10	5.10	1.76
Competence of workers	0.81	6.54	8	5	5.56	1.61
Customization of products	1.06	6.28	12	9	5.24	1.78
Convenient store entrance	1.18	6.00	14	15	4.35	1.81
Good in-store design	1.33	5.92	15	16	4.24	1.79
Parking close to store	1.53	5.59	16	19	3.85	2.09
Assortment	1.59	5.49	17	3	5.65	1.70
Frequently new products	1.55	5.45	18	13	4.45	1.80
Tastetests	1.50	5.29	19	22	2.97	2.00
Favorable offers	1.89	4.64	21	12	4.50	2.02
After sales service (delivery)	1.87	4.44	22	23	2.55	1.93
Rarely queue in store	1.82	4.09	23	14	4.40	1.90
Convenience food	2.04	3.33	24	24	2.15	1.66
Advertising in newspapers etc.	1.67	3.32	25	20	3.16	1.95
Low prices	1.43	3.25	26	17	4.17	1.92
Product ecology	1.70	3.10	27	18	3.39	1.87
Direct mail	1.84	2.90	28	21	3.12	1.99
Offering credit to customers	1.43	1.19	29	25	1.56	1.32
Special occasion				7	5.52	1.67
Competence of management	0.99	6.41	9			
Reliability of supplier delivery	0.91	6.40	10			
Good atmosphere among workers	0.89	6.38	11			
Customer loyalty	1.10	6.21	13			
Discount from suppliers	1.59	5.28	20			

From these points of view, it is surprising that specialty food store managers assign a relatively low priority to the 'assortment-factor' (scored 5.49, ranked 17) when designing their serviceoutput. Furthermore, it is difficult for supermarkets to posses specialized expertise in all the categories. The ability to provide specialized expertise is also one of the great advantages which specialty food stores traditionally enjoy over supermarkets (Levy & Weitz, 2001). According to the results displayed in Table 3 this factor seems still to be of importance. Specialty store managers attribute a high importance to the factor 'competence of workers' (6.54, ranked 8) when competing with supermarkets.

In Table 3 a distinction can be made between the factors concerning the *internal characteristics* of specialty stores and the factors concerning the *external characteristics* of specialty stores (Bamberger, 1989). The factors concerning the internal characteristics include competence of management (score 6.41, ranked 9), reliability of supplier delivery (score 6.40, ranked 10), good atmosphere among workers (score 6.38, ranked 11), and ability to get discounts from suppliers (5.28, ranked 20). Although these factors are not being directly exposed to customers they are nevertheless linked to the rest of the factors in Table 3, i.e. the external characteristics of the store. Specialty store managers can hardly obtain the desired level of the external characteristics without a certain level of the internal characteristics, and probably *vice versa*. As an example, it might be difficult to provide fresh products without having reliable suppliers. The results indicate that specialty store managers are aware of this way of reasoning since three out of four factors concerning the internal characteristics of specialty stores get a fairly high score/rank. Since 'low price' (scored 3.25, ranked 26) is not considered to be an important factor it is not surprising that the ability to get 'discounts from suppliers' (scored 5.28, ranked 20) gets the lowest score/rank of the four factors concerning the internal characteristics.

The evaluation of critical success factors may be influenced by the type of specialty food store in question. It is therefore interesting to look at the success factors when they are distributed over the four types of specialty food stores. The results of the applied ANOVA are presented in Table 4. The letters in parentheses indicate significant differences in the importance the stores attribute to the different factors.

A glance at Table 4 indicates that some differences exist between the four types of specialty food stores. Cheese-shops tend to place more weight on taste tests and low prices and less weight on high product quality and competence of workers. Baker's shops place more weight on a good in-store design whereas butcher's shops tend to place more weight on convenience food. Greengrocers assign a relatively low weight to in-store cleaning and competence of management. In general, specialty food store managers are, however, in agreement on most of the important factors (e.g. freshness of products, a good reputation, friendly workers, and a high service level). For these factors specialty food store managers are either in total agreement or in just minor disagreement.

Table 4. Specialty food store profiles

	All	A	B	C	D	Comparison of means
High product quality (a)	6.92	6.95	6.96	6.97	6.00	A=B=C>D
Freshness of products	6.91	6.87	6.98	6.96	6.75	
A good reputation (b)	6.81	6.79	6.87	6.36	6.96	D>C
Friendly workers	6.77	6.71	6.81	6.91	6.60	
High service level	6.76	6.82	6.76	6.82	6.95	
In-store cleaning (a)	6.75	6.63	6.96	5.70	6.97	A=B=D>C
Good in-store atmosphere	6.60	6.84	6.56	6.45	6.86	
Competence of workers (a)	6.54	6.78	6.48	6.55	5.00	A=B=C>D
Customization of products	6.28	6.27	6.22	6.45	6.38	
Convenient store entrance (a)	6.00	5.40	6.37	5.64	6.87	D>A=C
Good in-store design (a)	5.92	5.24	6.48	5.00	5.00	B>A=C=D
Parking close to store (a)	5.59	5.29	6.09	4.45	6.97	D>A=C; D=B>C
Assortment	5.49	4.92	5.65	6.09	6.00	
Frequently new products	5.45	4.78	5.80	5.55	5.05	
Tastetests (a)	5.29	4.54	5.49	4.82	7.00	D>A=B=C
Favorable offers	4.64	5.11	4.51	4.46	5.60	
After sales service (delivery)	4.44	4.08	4.63	5.45	4.07	
Rarely queue in store	4.09	3.92	4.26	4.27	3.52	
Convenience food (a)	3.33	4.60	3.14	2.10	1.00	A=B>D; A>C
Advertising in newspapers etc.	3.32	4.04	3.15	2.73	3.00	
Low prices (a)	3.25	3.42	2.91	4.55	6.68	D>A,B,C; C>B
Product ecology	3.10	2.36	3.10	3.55	4.00	
Direct mail	2.90	3.26	3.10	2.18	2.32	
Offering credit to customers	1.91	1.37	2.15	2.36	1.36	
Competence of management (a)	6.41	6.50	6.60	5.00	6.96	A=B=D>C
Reliability of supplier delivery	6.40	6.47	6.35	6.73	6.28	
Good atmosphere among workers	6.38	6.29	6.42	6.36	6.53	
Customer loyalty	6.21	6.08	6.28	6.27	6.76	
Discount from suppliers (b)	5.28	4.92	5.37	6.27	6.73	D>A

Notes: (a) prob.<0.01; (b) prob. <0.05. If noting else is stated means are statistically equal. A=Butcher's shops; B=Baker's shops; C=Greengrocer's shops; D=Cheese shops.

4.2 Research question 2: The importance assigned by consumers to store choice factors

In general, consumers' assigned importance to store choice factors correspond to store managers' evaluation of critical success factors (Table 3). A calculation of Spearman's rank correlation coefficient showed 0.82 indicating a rather high increasing relationship (similarity) between the two set of ranks. Only the factors included in both (a) and (b) were used in the calculation. The factors were therefore re-ranked before the calculation of the coefficient was carried out.

On average, consumers agree with managers that the two most important factors are high product quality (scored 6.11, ranked 2) and freshness of products (scored 6.14, ranked 1). Similar, low prices get a fairly low score by consumers (scored 4.17, ranked 17) indicating that both specialty food store managers and consumers do not view specialty food stores as 'discount stores'. There seems, however, to be a 'gap' between specialty store managers and consumers regarding the relative importance of assortment. While consumers rank this factor as number three (scored 5.65) specialty food store managers only rank the factor as number seventeen. Although there is an increasing demand for convenience food in the Danish marketplace (Munch, 2000) consumers do not claim that specialty food stores should add more convenience food (scored 2.15, ranked 24) to their assortment. It also seems that consumers do not consider specialty food stores as suppliers of 'product ecology' (scored 3.93, ranked 18). However, consumers do appreciate the ability of getting 'customized products' (scored 5.24, ranked 9). Also, consumers tend to be more likely to consider a specialty food store when they are shopping for a 'special occasion' (scored 5.52, ranked 7).

Recent research (Beatty et al., 1996; Reynolds & Arnold, 2000) suggests that interpersonal relationships between consumers and individual salespersons are related to store loyalty particular in those retail contexts where consumers prefer personalized service (e.g. specialty wine outlets; Macintosh & Lockshin, 1997). Relational selling behavior has also been found to affect perceived service quality, satisfaction, and purchase intentions (Crosby et al., 1990). In addition, Reynolds & Arnold (2000) argue, "social relationships may prompt customers to be more understanding when a service failure occurs" (p. 95). The results obtained in this study support the importance and value of individual salespersons in consumer store choice behavior. Consumers assign relatively high ranks to the factors 'friendly workers' (scored 5.47, ranked 8) and 'competence of workers' (scored 5.56, ranked 5).

4.3   Research question 3: Consumers' perceived image of specialty food stores

In total, consumers were asked to weigh 25 factors on the applied 7-point scale. It was investigated whether this relatively high number of factors could be reduced by applying principal components analysis, which is widely recognized as a method for datareduction (see e.g. Bagozzi, 1994). Bartlett's test of sphericity ($p < 0.0001$) and the Keyser-Meyer-Olkin measure of sampling adequacy of 0.886 indicated that the correlation matrix was appropriate for principal components analysis. The eigenvalue (>1)

criterion and the screetest both suggested a four-component solution (Table 5).

Table 5. Principal components analysis (consumer's opinion) (varimax rotation)

	Quality	Low price	Convenience	Shopping easiness
High product quality	0.812	0.030	0.181	-0.082
Freshness of products	0.732	0.038	0.161	-0.217
A good reputation	0.479	-0.016	0.359	0.215
Friendly workers	0.793	0.068	0.277	0.028
High service level	0.812	0.058	0.199	0.116
In-store cleaning	0.608	0.122	0.279	-0.021
Good in-store atmosphere	0.580	0.396	0.200	0.035
Competence of workers	0.806	-0.004	0.058	0.116
Customization of products	0.538	0.073	-0.056	0.143
Convenient store entrance	0.259	0.214	0.711	0.153
Good in-store design	0.327	0.258	0.583	0.163
Parking close to store	0.066	0.211	0.645	0.197
Assortment	0.547	0.100	0.121	-0.156
Frequently new products	0.330	0.446	0.350	0.078
Tastetests	0.203	0.042	0.082	0.657
Favorable offers	0.126	0.828	0.185	-0.009
After sales service (delivery)	0.142	0.058	0.210	0.703
Rarely queue in store	0.308	0.300	0.555	-0.090
Convenience food	-0.069	0.195	0.342	0.702
Advertising in newspapers	0.059	0.741	-0.003	0.415
Low prices	0.003	0.837	0.143	-0.006
Product ecology	0.097	-0.114	0.603	0.134
Direct mail	0.009	0.656	0.069	0.382
Offering credit to customers	-0.164	0.138	0.092	0.725
Special occasion	0.615	0.010	0.034	0.211
Cumulative variance (%)	30.5	44.6	51.7	56.7

The four dimensions were judgmentally labeled quality, low price, convenience, and shopping easiness. For the purpose of addressing research question 3, several aspects are now of interest.

1. Tables 3 and 4 show that specialty food store managers would like to picture themselves as suppliers of fresh, quality products complemented by a high and professional competence, among other factors. If this picture corresponds to consumers' overall perception of specialty food stores it should be expected that the higher the weights assigned to these factors (which are all included in dimension one, quality, refer to Table 5) by consumers, the more likely it is that consumers choose to shop in a specialty food store.

2. Managers assign little importance to the factors favorable offers, advertising in newspapers, low prices, and direct mail (refer to Tables 3 and 4). If this evaluation corresponds to consumers' perception of specialty food stores it should be expected that the higher the weights assigned to these factors (which are all included in dimension two, low price, refer to Table 5) by consumers, the less likely it is that consumers choose to shop in a specialty food store.

3. Tables 3 and 4 display that specialty food stores assign relatively little importance to factors like offering credit to consumers, direct mail, convenience food, after sales service, and taste tests. Again, if this evaluation corresponds to consumers' perception of store image it should be expected that the higher the weights assigned to these factors (which are all included in dimension four, shopping easiness, refer to Table 5) by consumers, the less likely it is that consumers choose to shop in a specialty food store.

4. Dimension three, 'convenience', (refer to Table 5) has not been put forward in the above review as this dimension consists mostly of average-ranked factors. Thus, it was not possible to make a priori suggestions of an either positive or negative effect of this dimension on consumer patronizing behavior. The conclusions drawn from (1), (2), and (3) may be moderated by a number of socioeconomic factors:

Income: Tables 3 and 4 indicate that people do not visit specialty food stores for the purpose of saving money. As per-household income rises, it might therefore be anticipated to be more likely that the consumers choose a specialty food store.

Age: Middle-aged and elderly people have been socialized with a specialty food store on almost 'every corner' and might therefore view specialty food store shopping as a more 'natural behavior' than do younger people. Thus as age rises in the dataset there should be expected a tendency to visit a specialty food store more often.

Amount spend on food: Because consumers do not visit specialty food stores to save money, i.e. specialty food stores are probably more expensive than supermarkets, there may be a tendency to visit a specialty food store more often as the amount spend on food in the household rises.

Number of persons in household: As the number of persons in a household rises, food could be expected to be bought in larger quantities, which do not favor specialty food stores.

General shopping frequency: A high general shopping frequency reflects most likely that a lot of time and effort is devoted to shopping. This could be expected to favor specialty food store shopping which is relatively time-consuming.

Not surprisingly, several major correlations were detected between the socioeconomic variables (e.g., between amount spend on food and size of household, $r=0.615$, prob. <0.001; and between size of household and income per year, $r=0.446$, prob. <0.001). A principal components analysis of the socioeconomic variables was therefore employed to minimize multicollinearity problems in the following analysis. Details of the principal components analysis are contained in the appendix (Table 9). A note about the dependent variable is also appropriate. It was considered to measure consumers store choice behavior (the dependent variable) as the percentage of total per-household food money spent in specialty food stores. However, because this percentage was very small for most households (on average less than five percent) this was given up due to lack of variation in the data. Instead, *shopping frequency* was employed as the dependent variable. Shopping frequency was measured by the consumer's response to the following statement: How often do you visit a specialty food store per month? The statement was measured on a six-point scale with end-points 'eight times or more' and 'less than one time' respectively.

Table 6. Regression results (consumer profiles)

Independent variable	Dependent variable	
	Shopping frequency	Shopping frequency
Choice criteria		
Quality	1.124 (a)	0.836 (a)
Low price	-0.412 (b)	-0.347
Convenience	0.186	-0.071
Shopping easiness	-0.391 (b)	-0.342
Socioeconomic variables		
Household size		-0.604 (a)
Age		-0.335 (b)
General shopping frequency		-0.826 (a)
R^2	0.112 (b)	0.187 (a)

Notes: No serious multicollinearity problems were detected between the
'choice-criteria' factors and the 'socioeconomic variables' factors.
(a) prob.<0.01; (b) prob.>0.05.

The results displayed in Table 6 show that the intended positioning of specialty food stores as suppliers of high quality food products corresponds to consumers' perceived image of the stores. Consumers who put high weight on quality are more likely to choose a specialty food store than are other consumers. This tendency holds true both with and without the socioeconomic variables although it is decreased a bit when the socioeconomic variables are taken into account. Consumers who put high priority on price are less likely to choose a specialty food store as compared to less price-sensitive consumers. This effect was, however, not significant when the effect of the socioeconomic variables was accounted for, although the negative sign of the regression coefficient is still maintained. Thus, consumers tend to perceive specialty food stores as providers of high priced high quality food products. Also, shopping easiness has negative coefficient signs, i.e. consumers who regard shopping easiness as an important factor tend to be less likely to choose a specialty food store. In total, only one of the socioeconomic variables (numbers of persons in household) came out with the predicted sign. Income and amount spent on food are both positively related to the factor 'household size' which in turn is negatively related to shopping frequency. One possible explanation is that specialty food shopping is time consuming and that high incomes may be complemented by strong limitations on the time available for shopping purposes. Also surprisingly, the last two socioeconomic variables, age and shopping frequency, had both negative, significant signs.

4.4   Research question 4: Future intertype competitiveness

Table 7 displays the results of the implementation of the three different measurements of competitiveness. Measurement 1 and 2 show values, which are significantly above the midpoint of each scale indicating that specialty store managers evaluate their own level of intertype competitiveness as being rather good. In measurement 3 only the total-value and the value obtained from the Baker's shops are significantly above the mid-point of the scale used in measurement 3. In sum, 12 of the 15 obtained values indicate, however, the presence of positive expectations towards future intertype competition.

Table 8 presents the results obtained from regressing the dependent variables (measurement 1, 2, and 3 respectively) on three characterizing variables: sales per year, distance to nearest supermarket, and distance to nearest specialty food store of the same type. As can be seen sales per year seems, not surprisingly, to have a positive influence on perceived competitiveness. Distance to nearest supermarket showed a significant negative effect on measurement 3. This indicates that specialty food stores might benefit from the presence of a supermarket in the same small local area, probably because a supermarket attracts consumers – some of which may choose to visit the specialty store also. The local presence of a specialty food store of the same type does not show a similar effect, probably because consumers seldom visit e.g. two baker's shops in one shopping trip.

Table 7. Managers' estimated future intertype competitiveness of specialty food stores

Respondents	Measurement 1 Mean	SD	Measurement 2 Mean	SD	Measurement 3 Mean	SD
Total	5.71 (a)	1.40	11.16 (a)	2.00	31.02 (a)	4.38
Greengrocer's shops	5.20 (a)	0.92	11.09 (a)	1.76	30.36	3.05
Butcher's shops	5.37 (a)	1.34	10.39 (a)	2.11	30.43	4.49
Baker's shops	5.85 (a)	1.51	11.40 (a)	2.00	31.57 (a)	4.21
Cheese shops	6.05 (a)	1.00	11.65 (a)	1.63	29.04	6.04

Notes: (a): prob < 0.01
(1) *Measurement 1* has a scale minimum of 1, a scale maximum of 7, and a scale mid-point of 4. *Measurement 2* has a scale minimum of 2, a scale maximum of 14, and a scale mid-point of 8. To avoid very large numbers *measurement 3* is divided by the number of competition factors (i.e. 29, see Table 3). This results in a scale minimum of 7, a scale maximum of 49, and a scale mid-point at 28.
(2) *Measurement 2:* Calculation of Cronbach's alpha for all respondents resulted in a value of 0.71, which is acceptable considering that the scale had only two items. Cronbach's alpha was for the individual types of shops 0.77 (greengrocer's shops), 0.68 (butcher's shops), 0.70 (baker's shops), and 0.79 (cheese-shops).
(a) display of the probability that a certain value minus its 'scale mid-point' is = 0).

Table 8. The moderating role of store characterizing variables

Independent variables	Dependent variables Measurement 1	Measurement 2	Measurement 3
Sales per year	0.184 (b)	0.272 (b)	0.241
Distance to nearest supermarket	0.093	0.043	-1.177 (a)
Distance to nearest specialty food store (of the same type)	-0.030	-0.067	-0.332
R²	0.046 (c)	0.048 (c)	0.101 (b)

Notes: (a) prob. <0.01; (b) prob. <0.05; (c) prob. < 0.10.

5. DISCUSSION

5.1 Implications

Specialty food stores have faced increased difficulties in competing with large supermarkets, which are able to offer not only competitive prices but also broad assortments and convenience. Being the case in many European countries (EIU, 1995) major Danish chains have improved their fresh food offerings in recent years and are now providing to a large degree what the specialty food stores have long done (MBI, 2000). The successful introduction of features such as in-store bakeries and fresh fish counters, along with an increasingly extensive fresh fruit and vegetables offer (EIU, 1995), have inevitably made matters much more difficult for specialty food stores. In short, specialty food stores have lost considerable share to supermarkets over the last decades. The results obtained in this paper strongly suggest, that specialty food stores should avoid competing on low costs with supermarkets. A struggle that specialty food stores nearly in advance would be deemed to loose. Instead, the results point out that freshness of products and high product quality should be given the highest priority.

However, the results of this research also indicate the presence of a 'gap' between consumers and managers regarding the assortment factor: managers assign a relatively low rank to the assortment factor whereas consumers regard assortment as an important determinant for their store choice behavior. This is unfortunate. Consumers could hereby become unsatisfied ('disconfirmed') as their expectations (or wants) may be higher than their perceptions of the delivered assortment (Neil et al., 2000; Szymanski & Heard, 2001). Previous research suggests that dissatisfied consumers could have a negative impact on ROI (Anderson et al., 1994); market share and profit (Fornell, 1992; Homburg & Rudolph, 2001), customer loyalty (Bearden & Teal, 1983; Kristensen et al., 2000), and overall firm performance (Anderson & Sullivan, 1993). Thus, specialty food store managers should adjust their in-store assortment in order to reduce the 'assortment-gap' and thereby reduce the risk that consumers become dissatisfied. However, the results suggest that these adjustments do not need to take into consideration the introduction of more convenience food or product ecology to the stores.

The results also indicate a correspondence between managers' intended store image and consumers' perceived store image. However, this does not imply that food managers should not monitor their store image carefully. Just like consumer preferences for various choice factors (Arnold et al., 1998), store image is not a static concept (Bell, 1999).

This study supports previous research (refer to Reynolds & Arnold, 2000) showing the importance of qualified and service-minded salespersons in building relationships to consumers. Indeed, evidence (Beatty et al., 1996) even suggests that consumers may follow a particular salesperson to another store with a corresponding merchandise should that salesperson changes her/his place of work. Thus, it is important that specialty food store salespersons receive continuous proper training in order to ensure professional competence and the ability to reveal consumer needs *and* that store managers foster an employee-friendly culture (Reynolds and Arnold, 2000).

The results also indicate, that consumers are more likely to choose a specialty food store if they are shopping for a special occasion. In the involvement literature (e.g. Antil, 1983; Ratchford, 1987) it is widely acknowledged that consumers generally feel a higher degree of involvement when they are purchasing food to be used for a special occasion (e.g., a guest situation) than when they are purchasing food to be used in a daily situation. Involved consumers can be expected to be more willing to devote resources (mental resources, time, and money) to the task they are going to perform than less involved consumers (refer to Celsi & Olson, 1988; Petty et al., 1983; Petty & Cacioppo, 1986). Thus, food store managers may have the opportunity of providing selling information which will not simply be neglected by consumers (Bettman, 1979; Petty & Cacioppo, 1986; Ceci & Loftus, 1994). As an example, specialty food store managers or sales personnel could refer to the potential negative health consequences of eating mass-produced food, and/or the positive effects of eating high quality food items.

5.2   Future research

As it is often the case in empirical research the results of this study rise more questions than they answer. As it is emphasized in the following a number of areas still need to be investigated in order to get a more comprehensive picture of the possibilities available for specialty food stores in order to improve their future intertype competitiveness. Foss & Knudsen (2000) argue that the "dominant contemporary approach to the analysis of sustained competitive advantage is the resource-based view" (p. 1). Resource-based theory takes the internal resource of a firm as unit of analysis in relation to the analysis of competitive advantages. It sees the internal resources of a firm as a key to understanding how to develop sustainable competitive advantages (e.g. Barney, 1991; Duncan et al., 1998). The resource-based perspective suggests that improved insight into the competitiveness of specialty food stores may be obtained by exploring the importance of leadership competencies and other internal resources and competencies like e.g. internal cost structure (Duncan et al., 1998).

According to Table 3 consumers and specialty food store managers seem to agree upon the most important competition/choice factors (Spearman's rank correlation coefficient being 0.82). In spite of this agreement, specialty food stores are still handing over marketshares to supermarkets (Table 2). This somewhat conflicting situation calls for a more thorough research with the purpose to uncover potential barriers, which might impede consumers from actually shop in specialty food stores. Perhaps consumer time-constraints (Munch, 2000) should be taken into account but also constraints originated in switching barriers (Jones, 2000), mental barriers in breaking up already established routines (e.g. Celsi & Olson, 1988; Howard & Sheth, 1969), and price barriers (Dodds et al., 1991; Chang & Wildt, 1994) may act as important shopping barriers. In connection hereto, the creation of superior product quality (Porter, 1980) or superior shopping value (Hazel, 1997; Duncan et al., 1998) should be considered as potential useful instruments for attracting consumers.

6.   CONCLUDING REMARKS

While specialty food stores have been reduced by numbers the remaining stores have increased their gross profit ratio. Also, there is to a large degree correspondence between the factors considered by specialty food store managers to be the most important intertype competition factors and the factors considered by consumers to be the most important for choosing a specialty food store instead of a supermarket. Moreover, consumers' perceived image of specialty food stores correspond to store managers' intended store image. Finally, specialty food store managers show very positive expectations towards future intertype competition with supermarkets. Thus, the results of this study seem to indicate that the days of specialty food stores are not over yet.

APPENDIX

Socioeconomic variables: Five socioeconomic variables were investigated: income, age, amount spend on food, number of persons in household, and general shopping frequency. Three factors were extracted from the data. They are shown in Table 9. Factor loadings in excess of ± 0.2 are reported. As can be seen, all factors are reasonably pure and their labels are obvious. These factors are the independent socioeconomic variables used as inputs in the regression results reported in Table 6 in the text.

Table 9. Principal components analysis (socioeconomic variables) (varimax rotation)

Variables	Factor labels		
	Household size	Age	Shopping freq.
Shopping frequency			0.968
Number of persons in household	0.871		
Amount spend on food	0.795	0.219	-0.275
Age of respondent		0.968	
Income (excl. taxes and allow.)	0.736		
Cumulative variance (%)	44.6	65.8	82.4

REFERENCES

Anderson, E.W., Fornell, C., Lehmann, D.R., 1994. Customer satisfaction, market share, and profitability: findings from Sweden, Journal of Marketing, Vol. 58, No. 3, pp. 53-66.

Anderson, E. W., Sullivan, M.W., 1993. The Antecedents and Consequences of Customer satisfaction for Firms, Marketing Science, 12 (2), pp. 125-143.

Antil, J.H., 1983. Conceptualization and Operationalization of Involvement, Advances in Consumer Research, pp. 203-209.

Arnold, S.J., Handelman, J., Tigert, D.J., 1996. Organizational Legitimacy and Retail Store Patronage, Journal of Business Research, 35, pp. 229-239.

Arnold, S.J., Handelman, J., Tigert, D.J., 1998. The impact of a market spoiler on consumer preference structures (or, what happens when Wal-Mart comes to town), Journal of Retailing and Consumer Services, Vol. 5, No. 1, pp. 1-13.

Bagozzi, R.P., 1994. Principles of Marketing Research, Blackwell.

Baker, M. J., Hart, S.J., 1989. Marketing and competitive success, Philip Allan.

Bamberger, I., 1989. Developing Competitive Advantages in Small and Medium-size Firms, Long Range Planning, Vol. 22, No. 5, pp. 80-88.

Barney, J.B., 1991. Firm Resources and Sustained Competitive Advantage, Journal of Management, 17, pp. 99-120.

Bearden, W.O., Teal, J.E., 1983. Selected Determinants of Consumer Satisfaction and Complaint Reports, Journal of Marketing Research, Vol. XX, February, pp. 21-28.

Beatty, S.E., Mayer, M.L., Coleman, J.E., Reynolds, K.E, Lee, J., 1996. Customer-Sales Associate Retail Relationships, Journal of Retailing, 72, pp. 223-247.

Bell, S.J., 1999. Image and consumer attraction to interurban retail areas: An environmental psychology approach, Journal of Retailing and Consumer Services, 6, pp. 67-78.

Bettman, J.R., 1979. Information processing theory of consumer choice, Reading, Mass.

Ceci, S.J., Loftus, E.F., 1994. Memory Work: A Royal Road to False Memories, Applied Cognitive Psychology, Vol. 8, pp. 351-364.

Celsi, R. L., Olson, J.C., 1988. The role of involvement in attention and comprehension processes, Journal of Consumer Research, Vol. 15, pp. 210-224.

Chang, T.Z., Wildt, A.R., 1994. Price, product information, and purchase intention; An empirical study, Journal of the Academy of Marketing Science, Vol. 22, pp. 16-27.

Collins, A., 1992. Competitive retail marketing, McGraw-Hill Book Company.

Crosby, L.A., Evans, K.R., Cowles, D., 1990. Relationship Quality in Services Selling: An Interpersonal Influence Perspective, Journal of Marketing, 54, pp. 68-81,

Dodds, W.B., Monroe, K.B., Grewal, D., 1991. Effects of Price, Brand, and Store Information on Buyers' Product Evaluations, Journal of Marketing Research, Vol. 28, pp. 307-319.

DS., 1985. Statistisk Ti-årsoversigt 1985, The Danish Statistical Bureau.

DS., 2000. Statistisk Ti-årsoversigt 2000, The Danish Statistical Bureau.

Duncan, J.W., Ginter, P.M., Swayne, L.E., 1998. Competitive advantage and internal organizational assessment, Academy of Management Executive, Vol. 12, No. 3, pp. 6-16.

EIU, The Economist Intelligence Unit Limited, 1995. Specialist food shops, Retail Trade Review, No. 36.

Engel, J.E., Blackwell, R.D., Kegerreis, R.J., 1969. How Information Is Used to Adopt an Innovation, Journal of Advertising Research

Finn, A., Louviere, J.J., 1996. Shopping Center Image, Consideration, and Choice: Anchor Store Contribution, Journal of Business Research, 35, pp. 241-251.

Fornell, C., 1992. A national customer satisfaction barometer: The Swedish experience, Journal of Marketing, Vol. 56, No. 1, pp. 6-21.

Foss, N.J., Knudsen, T., 2000. The Resource-Based Tangle: Towards a Sustainable Explanation of Competitive Advantage, Working Paper 2000-1, Department of Industrial Economics and Strategy, Copenhagen Business School.

Hair, J.F. Jr., Bush, R.P., Ortinau, D.J., 2000. Marketing Research, McGraw-Hill International Editions.

Hazel, D., 1997. Is Value Retail Lossing its Focus?, Chain Store Age, May, pp. 75-78.

Hildebrandt, L., 1988. Store Image and the Prediction of Performance in Retailing, Journal of Business Research, 17, pp. 91-100.

Hise, R.T., Kelly, J.P., Gable, M., McDonald, J.B., 1983. Affecting the Performance of Individual Chain Store Units. An Empirical Analysis, Journal of Retailing, 59, pp. 22-39.

Hofer, C.W., Schendel, D., 1983. Strategy formulation: Analytical concepts, St. Paul, Minn., West Publishing Company.

Homburg, C., Rudolph, B., 2001. Customer satisfaction in industrial markets: dimensional and multiple role issues, Journal of Business Research, 52, pp. 15-33.

Howard, J.A., Sheth, J.N., 1969. The Theory of Buyer Behavior, New York, Wiley.

Ingene, C.A., 1983. Intertype Competition: Restaurants versus Grocery Stores, Journal of Retailing, Vol. 59, No. 3, pp. 49-75.

Jones, M.A., 2000. Switching barriers and repurchase intentions in services, Journal of Retailing, Vol. 76, Iss. 2, pp. 259-274.

Kristensen, K., Martensen, A., Grønholdt, L., 2000. Measuring customer satisfaction: a key dimension of business performance, International Journal of Business Performance Management, Vol. 2, No. 1/2/3, pp. 157-170.

Larsen, H.H., 1996. Udviklingen i detailhandlen – lighedspunkter og forskelle landene imellem, notat, Handelshøjskolen i København.

Leszczyc, P.T.L.P., Sinha, A., Timmermans, H.J.P., 2000. Consumer Store Choice Dynamics: An Analysis of the Competitive Market Structure for Grocery Stores, Journal of Retailing, Vol. 76(3), pp. 323-345.

Levy, M., Weitz, B.A., 2001. Retailing Management, 4th ed. Boston: Irwin McGraw-Hill.

Macintosh, G., Lockshin, L., 1997. Retail Relationships and Store Loyalty: A Multi-Level Perspective, International Journal of Research in Marketing, 5, pp. 487-497.

Marion, B.W., 1998. Competition in Grocery Retailing: The Impact of a New Strategic Group on BLS Price Increases, Review of Industrial Organization, 13, pp. 381-399.

Martilla, J.A., 1971. Word-of-Mouth Communication in the Industrial Adoption Process, Journal of Marketing Research, 8, pp. 173-178.

Martineau, P., 1958. The personality of the retail store, Harvard Business Review, 36, pp. 47-55.

Mazursky, D., Jacoby, J., 1986. Exploring the Development of Store Images, Journal of Retailing, 62, pp. 145-165.

MBI., 2000. Konkurrenceredegørelse 2000, The Danish Competitive Authority, The Danish Ministry of Business and Industry.

Miller, C.E., Reardon, J., McCorkle, D.E., 1999. The Effects of Competition on Retail Structure: An Examination of Intratype, Intertype, and Intercategory Competition, Journal of Marketing, Vol. 63, pp. 107-120.

Munch, J., 2000. Det er ikke sjovt at skrælle kartofler, Aktuelt, 10 October, p. 3.

Myers, J.H., Robertson, T.S., 1972. Dimensions of Opinion Leadership, Journal of Marketing Research, 9, February, pp. 41-46.

Nield, K., Kozak, M., LeGrys, G., 2000. The role of food service in tourist satisfaction, International Journal of Hospitality Management, 19, pp. 375-384.

Parasuraman, A., Zeithaml, V., Berry, L., 1985. A Conceptual Model of Service Quality and Its Implications for Future Research, Journal of Marketing, 49, pp. 41-50.

Petty, R.E., Cacioppo, J.T., Schumann, D., 1983. Central and Peripheral Routes to Advertising Effectiveness: The Moderating Role of Involvement, Journal of Consumer Research, Vol. 10, pp. 135-146.

Petty, R.E., Cacioppo, J.T., 1986. The Elaboration Likelihood Model of Persuasion, Advances in Experimental Social Psychology, Vol. 19, 123-205.

Porter, M., 1979. The Structure within Industries and Companies' Performance, Review of Economics and Statistics, 61, pp. 214-227.

Porter, M., 1980. Competitive Strategy, The Free Press.

Ratchford, B.T., 1987. New Insight About the FCB Grid, Journal of Advertising Research, Vol. 27, pp. 24-37.

Reynolds, K.E., Arnold, M.J., 2000. Customer Loyalty to the Salesperson and the Store: Examining Relationship Customers in an Upscale Retail Context, Journal of Personal Selling & Sales Management, Vol. XX, No. 2, pp. 89-98.

Rigby, P.E., 1998. Trends in retailing, Commercial Lending Review, Vol. 13, Iss. 1, pp. 7-9.

Rockart, J.F., 1979. Chief Executives Define Their Own Data Needs, Harvard Business Review, 57, pp. 81-93.

Sheth, J.N., Eshghi, A., Krishnan, B.C., 2001. Internet Marketing, Harcourt College Publishers.

Sirgy, J.M., Grewal, D., Mangleburg, T., 2000. Retail Environment, Self-Congruity, and Retail Patronage: An Integrative Model and a Research Agenda, Journal of Business Research, 49, pp. 127-138.

Solomon, M., Bamossy, G., Askegaard, S. 1999. Consumer Behavior, Prentice Hall Europe.

SOU, Statens offentliga utredningar., 1994. Konsumenterna och livsmedelskvaliteten - En studie av konsumentupplevelser, delbetänkande av Konsumentberedningen, Stockholm.

Steenkamp, J.B.E.M., Van Trijp, H.C.M., 1989. Quality guidence: A consumer-based approach for product quality improvement. In: Marketing Thought and Practice in the 1990s, ed. G.J. Avlonitis, N.K. Papavasilliou & A.G. Kouremenos, pp. 1191-1217.

Stern, L.W., El-Ansary, A.I., 1988. Marketing Channels, Prentice-Hall, Inc.

Stockmann, 1999. Supermarkedshåndbogen, Stockmann-Gruppen A/S.

Stockmann, 2000. Supermarkedshåndbogen, Stockmann-Gruppen A/S.

Szymanski, D.M., Henard, D.H., 2001. Customer Satisfaction: A Meta-Analysis of the Empirical Evidence, Journal of the Academy of Marketing Science, Vol. 29, No. 1, pp. 16-35.

Urbany, J.E., Dickson, P.R., Key, R., 1991. Actual and Perceived Consumer Vigilance in the Retail Grocery Industry, Marketing Letters, 2, pp. 15-25.

Urbany, J.E., Dickson, P.R., Sawyer, A.G., 2000. Insights Into Cross- and Within-Store Price Search: Retailer Estimates Vs. Consumer Self-Reports, Journal of Retailing, Vol. 76(2), pp. 243-258.

Wilcox, M., O'Callaghan, E., 2001. The strategic response of Dublin's traditional department stores to intensifying competition, Journal of Retailing and Consumer Services, 8, pp. 213-225.

Chapter 7

EPILOGUE

1.   INTRODUCTION

Retailing and consumer store choice behavior constitute fascinating research areas within the field of marketing. Retailing contributes to an increasing proportion of gross national products and employment but is, however, also faced with problems and opportunities like increased product complexity, rapidly changing consumer expectations, and the introduction of new technologies. Also, consumers are facing markets of increasingly complexity when making decisions on how to conduct their behavior, primarily as a result of new technologies, shorter products life cycles in general, and higher complexity of products and services.

In this book, we have presented and dealt with various topics in relation to retailing and consumer store choice behavior. Together, these topics involve different problem settings and draw on different theories, models and statistical techniques. However, it is common to all the results presented in the preceding chapters (with the exception of chapter II) that they, in total or in part, rest on a major survey, which was conducted by the authors in 2000. The details of the survey have been outlined in chapter I. Minor descriptions of the survey design may also be found in the individual chapters, which constitute the body of this book. We have chosen this method of presentation to allow readers interested in just one or few of the chapters to focus on these without having to read the introductory chapter or other chapters.

The major purpose of the present book has not been to write a 'textbook'. Excellent textbooks covering the many facets of retailing and consumer store choice do already exist (e.g., Levy and Weitz, 2001). Instead, our main purpose has been to provide an in-depth investigation and discussion of some selected topics, which in our opinion are among the more interesting and evolving contemporary topics within the field of retailing and consumer store choice behavior. In this final chapter, we consider a number of additional topics, which we believe will receive increasingly importance and consideration by research and retail management. In relation to each topic we provide suggestions for future research.

2.   CONSTRUCTIVE CONSUMER DECISION MAKING

The increasingly shortened life cycle of many products, the increasing internationalization and complexity as well as the emergence of the Internet are all examples of conditions that have contributed to the fact that the environment in which the consumer must plan and execute her/his behavior has become increasingly complex. As noted by Bettman et al. (1998) one approach to studying consumer decision making has been to assume a rational decision maker with well-defined preferences. Another perspective, the information perspective, emphasizes that consumers have limitations on their capacity for processing information. These limitations include limited working memory and limited computational capabilities (Hansen, 1972; Bettman et al., 1998). Since the consumer's processing capacity is limited, the consumer cannot process high amounts of cognitive information in relation to all choice situations. This view suggests that in many choice situations consumers are faced with bounded rationality. Bounded rationality can be seen either as the attempt to do as well as possible given the demands of the world – the notion of optimization under constraints – or as the suboptimal outcome of the limited cognitive system (cf. Todd and Gigerenzer, 2003).

The increasing complexity of the marketplace together with the notion of bounded rationality suggests that consumers are not always capable of perceiving and evaluating all relevant market and product attributes and that consumers do not always posses well-defined preferences for all choice problems. In some choice situations consumers may instead 'construct' their preferences on 'the spot' rather than referring to a master list of preferences in memory (Gregory et al., 1993; Bettman et al., 1998). Examples of such choice situations may include situations in which consumers lack the competences necessary for developing preferences for various attributes and/or situations in which consumers bring multiple goals to a given decision problem. A consumer who wants to buy a basket of 'healthy' food products in a supermarket may be uncertain on what food product attributes to prefer to fulfill that goal. The consumer may try to overcome the uncertainty and the possible lack of food competence by selecting one or more indicators (e.g., high price, a brand with which s/he is confident, etc.) as a basis for the assessment of the healthiness of the food products. In other incidents the consumer may try to minimize the cognitive dissonance, which may result from not knowing the 'right' decision, by ignoring, or even denying, that food products are heterogeneous with respect to their healthiness. For example, the consumer can 'decide' that no food products legally offered in the marketplace are unhealthy and thereby trust that food authorities are doing a good and restrictive job when monitoring the marketplace. Such a consumer may simply buy a basket consisting of low priced food items and then justifying her/his decision making by referring to the amount of money that has been saved. However, if the consumer's future food competences improve (and the goal of being healthy remains unchanged) the consumer may change her/his way of decision making and engage in extensive comparisons of various food products. As a consequence, the consumer may end up preferring food items, which are medium-priced or high-priced. Thus, as noted by Bettman et al. (1998) consumer decision making will be highly sensitive to the local problem structure. Another characteristics of constructive decision making is that most often it is contingent although contingent decision making does not necessarily constitute constructive decision making, i.e., when preferences are developed on the spot. For example, a consumer may have a well-established, but contingent, preference for red wine in combination with red meat and a preference for white wine in combination with a fish-menu. Such preferences are not constructive (Bettman et al., 1998).

When consumers make a decision they must trade-off the desire to make a reasonable decision with the resources (mental resources, time, and money) they are using in relation to the decision making process, i.e., a 'cost-benefit' approach (refer to Payne, 1982). Several specific consumer decision making strategies have been considered in the literature including weighted adding, lexicographic strategy, and elimination by aspects. These decision making strategies can be characterized according to the total amount of information processed, the selectivity in the information processing, the pattern of processing, and whether the strategy is compensatory or not compensatory (Bettman et al., 1998). Thus, the selection of a specific decision making strategy should be considered in combination with the above-mentioned trade-off between the desire to make a reasonable decision and the resources used to reach a decision. It can be expected that the selection of a specific decision making strategy will vary depending on the construction of the trade-off; e.g., depending on the weights the consumer assigns to the trade-off components. Bettman et al. have proposed a choice goals framework, which integrates the cost-benefit approach with a perceptual approach. The perceptual approach mainly deals with what aspects of a choice of task that are noticed by the consumer and how these tasks are represented. The cost-benefit (accuracy-effort) can be used as a basic perspective for considering how consumers utilize noticed information in order to fulfill their goals. In our opinion the proposed framework represents a promising tool for developing a more thoroughly understanding of consumer constructive decision making. In the following we briefly outline the main aspects and considerations of the framework. Next, we discuss the implications for research and practice.

A main aspect of the Bettman et al. framework is that choices are made to achieve goals. Three basic goals are detected in the framework: (1) choice situations where accuracy and effort goals dominate, (2) choice situations where minimizing negative emotion is relevant, and (3) choice situations where maximizing ease of justification is relevant. Bettman et al. propose that accuracy and effort goals dominate in situations where there is little consumer involvement or need to justify, whereas consumers may seek to minimize negative emotion in situations involving choice conflicts between the accomplishments of perceived important goals. Ease of justification may especially be relevant in situations that are more perceptual in nature. The Bettman et al. framework highlights that consumers have a repertoire of decision making strategies, which may vary according to characteristics concerning the individual consumer (e.g., experience, competencies, age), the situations (e.g., time pressure, social visibility of the decision) and the product (e.g., product complexity, price). In relation to each of the three depicted choice situations Bettman et al. suggest a number a propositions, which summarizes how consumers may behave in more detail in connection to attaining the choice goal. Some examples of the propositions are: (1) Choice tasks where accuracy and effort goals dominate: Increases in the number of alternatives lead to a greater use of noncompensatory choice strategies. Increases in the number of attributes generally lead to increased selectivity, but not to strategy changes. (2) Choice tasks where minimizing negative emotion is relevant: Emotion-laden choices are characterized by more extensive, more selective, and more attribute-based processing. In general, emotion-laden choices encourage avoidant behaviors. (3) Choice tasks where maximizing ease of justification is relevant: Adding an asymmetrically dominated alternative to a choice set results in increased choice share for the dominating alternative. This effect is enhanced under increased need for justification. Readers are encouraged to see the Bettman et al. article for a further discussion of the propositions. The Bettman et al. framework certainly points to a number of important aspects, which we believe will receive increased intention by future research and future retail management:

What factors determine consumers' selection of choice goals? How can retailers influence the selection process?

What types of information do consumers use when constructing preferences? How do consumers overcome missing information, information that is difficult to understand, unreliable information, and/or ambiguous information?

3. A NEGATIVE QUALITY SPIRAL?

An increasing number of different foods and variants in the marketplace probably means that the battle between high quality food producers, who wish to make it possible for the consumers to distinguish between high and low qualities, and low quality food producers, who wish to slur the quality differences, becomes more uneven. This may happen, as the increased market complexity most likely is an advantage for low quality food producers. As a result of the increased market complexity and the larger degree of uncertainty, it will be easier for these producers, and their connected retailers, to give the impression that the products in a given product category are more homogenous than the competing high quality suppliers would most likely argue. This is an advantage for low quality producers, as their cost levels are usually lower than high quality producers'. If the low quality producers succeed in convincing the increasingly uncertain consumers that there are no significant differences between the supplied food variants on the market, this would leave the consumer with only one thrifty alternative: to purchase the cheapest foods, i.e. those supplied by the low quality producers!

If they succeed on a large scale, and the market is gradually convinced that there are no significant differences between the substituting foods on the market, competitors with higher cost levels may be forced to lower these. This will eventuate if the competitors are unable to explain to and convince the market that higher priced foods bring more and/or greater benefits and thus more value to the consumer. This is getting increasingly difficult. Therefore, the focus on price could release a negative quality spiral, which, in the long run, would benefit some consumers – those who are already more or less exclusively focused on price – but would greatly harm others – those who want high quality products and who, to some degree, are able to discern quality – as the supply of high quality products on the food market would be gradually reduced resulting from the negative quality spiral. A number of questions arise in connection to such considerations.

To what extend can the 'negative quality spiral' be detected empirically in consumer food markets? How will high quality producers react to a 'negative quality spiral'? What strategies should be implemented? What will be done by food producers and/or retailers to help consumers to discern quality? What are the implications for the food culture in a society with a 'negative quality spiral'?

4.   CHANGE OF THE MUTUAL SCARCITY OF CONSUMER RESOURCES

The consumers' resources (time, money and mental resources) are all scarce. However, the mutual scarcity of resources has changed in the past couple of years. The consumers' money has become relatively less scarce, while the time and mental resources we are willing to use considering each individual purchase have become relatively scarcer. This is not due to time and mental resources becoming scarcer, rather the activities that we pass time with have increased in number and complexity. Thus, consumers are forced to prioritize their use of resources for all activities, including shopping for goods. In this connection, some goods may be categorized as relatively readily available 'functional goods' (e.g. flour, oats, toilet paper, freezing bags etc.) that rarely give us any particular pleasure when shopping for or using them. Other goods are characterized as hedonic ('pleasurable') (e.g. clothes, wine, specialty cheeses etc.) that often bring us pleasure when shopping for and consuming them. When comparing this definition of goods, which goes against the more commonly known division into groceries and shopping goods, to the fact that time has become more important than money, the result is significant for the retailer. As an example, lets look at a supermarket. According to the above, a common supermarket is in reality two stores in one, but is rarely designed accordingly. As far as the functional goods are concerned, the consumers will be looking to save time and for readily available information. In the case of pleasure goods, the consumers will be more willing to spend time and mental resources (while perhaps lacking the competences to fully appreciate the goods). The consequences of these considerations for the supermarket are obvious. The consumer should be given the possibility of reducing or even allocating the time spent shopping for functional goods (e.g. by pre-ordering via the Internet or by paying for pre-picking and packing at the store). In connection with the pleasure goods, the consumer should be given the possibility of access to expert help and to exciting and inviting displays. Taking it to the extreme, the supermarket would thus be divided into two departments; a functional department (where the interior would reflect the wish for quick and well-planned access to goods) and a pleasure department (where the interior reflects the wish for inviting displays and a focus on the pleasure side of things). In relation hereto, future research may wish to address the following questions.

What are the possible implications of the change in the mutual scarcity of consumer resources for the design of future supermarkets?

How can retail managers help consumers to overcome scarce resources?

5. CONSUMERS' ROLE PLAY

A consumer is exposed to, finds her/himself in and participates in a large number of situations. The playing of such roles helps define the consumer in relation to her/his surroundings to a very high degree, both regarding the individual's own self-perception and the social environment's understanding of the consumer. The understanding, however, does change over time. We play different roles – that may change radically in the course of a day – and in the course of a lifetime. The consumer can exist simultaneously as a citizen and consumer and in this capacity take on a number of supporting roles. Like an actor who changes scene or play, the consumer changes between different situations and expressions. The individual consumer's freedom in connection with this 'role play', however, is not unlimited and in many situations s/he must more or less conform to the existing rules. As modern man participates in increasingly diverse situations and has access to more material resources, it has become more difficult to establish consistent norms, just as the economic and cultural freedom (and thus the individual responsibility) to create an individual expression has become greater. Thus, consumers should not only be viewed as passive carriers of different roles, or as passive expectations of values and expectations. Consumers do not simply live up to a predetermined 'set of rules'. Our identity and our understanding of the world around us are not created solely by simple replication or reproduction of existing standards and behavioral patterns, but may also reflect a 'struggle' to improve these standards and behavioral patterns in the attempt to obtain self-satisfaction. In relation hereto, a distinction can be made between social values and personal values. Social values define the 'normal' behavior for a society or group, whereas personal values define the 'normal' behavior for an individual (refer to Blackwell et al., 2001). Based on such considerations, we suggest as follows.

To analyse, describe and understand these complex contexts represents a great challenge for the retailer; the challenge lies not least in determining how the consumer might use the retailer's goods in her/his choice of roles. The retailer not only represents a store containing goods, the store and goods also play a role in the consumer's self-dramatization process, i.e. the store and goods also have a communicative expression via the individual consumer and the way in which the goods are used in social contexts.

6.   INTERNET RETAILING AND CONSUMERS' ONLINE PURCHASE INTENTIONS

Previous research (refer to Hansen, 2003) suggests that music, videos and books, travels and vacation, PC-supplies, tickets, flowers/gifts, and clothes are the most popular online consumer goods. In general, a large search activity is taking place on the Internet. In a study of Danish and Swedish online consumers (Hansen, 2003) more than one third of the respondents have sought online information for most consumer products. A problem arises, however, when one looks at the propensity to buy online as compared to the propensity to seek information online. For example, in Denmark 41% of online consumers have sought online information concerning groceries but only 7% have actually made an online grocery buying. In Sweden, the corresponding figures 51% and 10%, respectively (all figures are from fall 2002). Recognizing that some online information seeking may not be buying-oriented such results suggest, nevertheless, that many consumers have an open mind towards the idea of combining (at least some part of) their grocery buying process with the Internet channel. However, there seems to be some obstacles present, which prevent consumers from 'going all the way' and actually make, for example, an online grocery buying. Such considerations hold also true in relation to a lot of other consumer products, e.g. household goods and articles, PCs, furniture, medicine, personal care items, etc. In general, many theories (and in relation hereto theoretical concepts) have been put forwards in trying to explain why consumers seem to be more likely to buy some products as compared to other products and why some products are nearly avoided by online consumers (in Denmark and Sweden such products include furniture, medicine, and long-term accommodation). Two of those theories are broadly considered here.

It has been advanced that a consumer will choose the online (or offline) shop that according to the consumer offers the greatest value (Sweeney and Soutar, 2001; Harnett, 1998). In relation hereto, two basic types of 'shopping value' can be identified (refer to e.g., Babin et al., 1994; Childers et al., 2001): (1) an utilitarian shopping value, which can be related to the consumer's need to obtain some utilitarian consequences, i.e., a product or service, from visiting a store. This behavior can also be referred to as 'problem solving behavior' (Hirshman and Holbrook, 1982). (2) However, consumers may also choose among retailers from a need to obtain a hedonic shopping value. The hedonic shopping value refers to the consumer's need to gain feelings through senses and to obtain emotional arousal. In this connection, the Internet is often described as an interactive media or channel that allows consumers to take control of the exchange information between marketers and consumers (Storm, 2001; Hoffman and Novak, 1996). In relation hereto, it is hypothesized that the consumer wants "convenience, speed, comparability, (low) price, and service" (Sampler and Hamel, 1998, p. 54). Thus, the consumer is expected to stress a utilitarian shopping value, which suggests that consumers mainly will be interested in buying utilitarian products via the Internet. However, evidence (refer to Hansen, 2003; Hansen and Jensen, 2003) suggests that such considerations are insufficient in explaining consumer online purchasing behavior. For example, clothes, flowers, and vacation are among the most popular online products in both Denmark and Sweden.

The 'economics of information approach' (refer to Nelson, 1970; Steenkamp, 1989) argues that the main problem for the consumer is to evaluate the utility of each product alternative. Nelson proposed two methods for evaluating the utility of product: search and experience. Search refers to the actual inspection of the product prior to purchase to evaluate its utility. A consumer can search for quality as well as price. For many products, however, search is not possible or is too expensive. Two kinds of product-types can now be identified (credence goods are not considered here) (Peterson et al., 1997; Alba et al., 1997): search products: products for which a major part of the perceived relevant attributes can be assessed prior to purchase; experience products, products for which a major part of the relevant attributes is difficult to asses prior to purchase. It has been suggested (refer to Peterson et al., 1997) that products selected by consumers primarily on the basis of search attributes are most amenable to online retailing because direct experience is not required. In both Denmark and Sweden, 5 out of the top 6 ranked products (in relation to online buying) can be classified as search products (music/videos/books, travels/vacation, tickets, PC supply, and flowers) (Hansen, 2003). From an economics of information perspective this result suggest that for many online products consumers are simply imperfectly informed and may therefore hesitate to move on to an online buying. One may therefore be tempted to conclude that search products are most suitable for online retailing. However, such a conclusion may be a simplistic representation of the problem, as it does not take into account the primary reason why consumers engage in information search activities, namely to reduce risk. The main problem seems instead to be whether it is possible to provide consumers with information that compensates for the lack of direct product information in relation to online experience products. At least two possibilities exist in this connection: (1)

To provide information, which in the eyes of the consumer can substitute direct product information (search information) and thereby reduce consumers' perceived purchase risk. (2) To provide consumers with 'risk releavers' (Van den Poel and Leunis, 1999), which may reduce the perceived post-purchase risk. In addition hereto, recent research (Kivetz and Simonson, 2000; Simonson, 1999) suggests that a number of psychological principles underlie consumer choice behavior when choice are made under uncertainty. One such principle is the need for 'justification', which may arise in situations where the consumer lacks information (qualitative information and/or quantitative information), lacks the necessary competence to process the information and/or are unwilling to invest enough resources in the information search process. The principle of justification may result in the consumer developing preference for relatively superior options; preference for compromise options; avoiding cheapest option; delaying choice when a consideration set involves multiple attractive options (refer to Simonson, 1999). Another psychological principle, which may help understand consumer choice behavior under uncertainty, is the 'ease of processing principle'. This principle suggests that consumers emphasize easy to compare attributes when evaluating several options simultaneously, and emphasize attributes for which all options have known values (cf. Simonson, 1999). Based on the above discussion future research may wish to deal with the following questions.

What kind of decision rules do online consumers apply for various products and services?

How can online retailers lower consumers' perceived purchase risk and/or post-purchase risk? What factors constitute consumers' perceived risk?

REFERENCES

Alba, J., Lynch, J., Wietz, B., Janiszewski, C., Lutz, R., Sawyer, A. and Wood, S. (1997), Interactive Home Shopping: Consumer, Retailer, and Manufacturer Incentives to Participate in the Electronic Marketplace, Journal of Marketing, Vol. 61, pp. 38-53.

Babin B. J., Darden W. R. and Griffin M. (1994), Work and/or Fun: Measuring Hedonic and Utilitarian Shopping Value, Journal of Consumer Research, 20, 4, 644-656.

Bettman, J.R., Luce, M.F and Payne, J.W. (1998), Constructive Consumer Choice Processes, Journal of Consumer Research, Vol. 25, December, pp. 187-217.

Childers T. L., Carr C. L., Peck J. and Carson S. (2001), Hedonic and utilitarian motivations for online retail shopping behavior, Journal of Retailing, 77, 511-535.

Gregory, R., Lichtenstein, S., and Slovic, P. (1993), Valuing Environmental Resources: A Constructive Approach, Journal of Risk and Uncertainty, 7 (Octorber), pp. 177-197.

Hansen, F. (1972), Consumer Choice Behavior - A Cognitive Theory, The Free Press/ McMillan, New York and London.

Hansen, T. (2003), The Online Grocery Consumer: Results From Two Scandinavian Surveys, Working Paper No. 1, March, Department of Marketing, Copenhagen Business School.

Hansen, T. and Jensen, J.M. (2003), Predicting Consumer Online Buying Intention: A Conceptual Model Tested on Five Product Categories, Paper presented at the 1st International Conference on Business, Economics, Management and Marketing, Athens, June 26-29.

Harnett, M. (1998), Shopper Needs Must Be Priority, Discount Store News, 37, pp. 21-22.

Hirschman E. and Holbrook M. B. (1982), Hedonic Consumption: Emerging Concepts, Methods and Propositions, Journal of Marketing, 46, 92-101.

Hoffman, D.L. and Novak, T.P. (1996), Marketing in Hypermedia Computer-Mediated Environments: Conceptual Foundations, Journal of Marketing, Vol. 60, July, pp. 50-68.

Kivetz, R. and Simonson, I. (2000), The Effects of Incomplete Information on Consumer Choice, Journal of Marketing Research, Vol. XXXVII, pp. 427-448.

Levy, M. and Weitz, B.A. (2001), Retailing management, 4ed. Irwin, Boston, Mass.

Nelson, P. (1970), Information and consumer behavior, Journal of Political Economy, 78, pp. 311-329.

Payne, J.W. (1982), Contingent Decision Behavior, Psychological Bulletin, 92 (September), pp. 382-402.

Peterson, R.A., Balasubramanian, S, and Rosenberg, B.J. (1997), Exploring the Implications of the Internet for Consumer Marketing, Journal of the Academy of Marketing Science, Vol. 25, No. 4, pp. 329-346.

Sampler, J. and Hamel, G. (1998), The E-Corporation, Fortune, Vol. 7, December, pp. 52-63.

Steenkamp, J.B.E. M. (1989), Product Quality, Van Corcum, The Netherlands.

Simonson, I. (1999), The Effect of Product Assortment on Buyer Preferences, Journal of Retailing, Vol. 75 (3), pp. 347-370.

Storm, D. (2001), Telling Tales of the Consumer in Cyberspace – a phenomenological study of online shopping experiences, Working Paper No. 27/September, Department of Marketing, University of Southern Denmark, Odense.

Sweeney, J.C., Soutar, G.N., and Johnson, L.W. (1999), The Role of Perceived Risk in the Quality-Value Relationship: A Study in a Retail Environment, Journal of Retailing, Vol. 75(1), pp. 77-105.

Todd, P.M. and Gigerenzer, G. (2003), Bounded rationality to the world, Journal of Economic Psychology, Volume 24, Issue 2, pp. 143-165.

Van den Poel, D. and Leunis, J. (1999), Consumer Acceptance of the Internet as a Channel of
    Distribution, Journal of Business Research, 45, pp. 249-256.

Index